T0381364

Brassavola cordata Orchid, (Lady of the Night) nestled in the filtered shade of a moss-covered orange tree

www.trafford.com

North America & international
toll-free: 1 888 232 4444 (USA & Canada)
phone: 250 383 6864 ♦ fax: 812 355 4082

GARDENING PASSION

Resourceful gardening information. Intimately cultivated and lavishly photographed for your pleasure.

FORLET BRIGHT GRAY

A lush water garden with a constant movement of water maintained by a solar pump.

It is inhabited by numerous aquatic animals and is the home of many aquatic plants

ISBN – 9781490767116

Copyright

Forlet Bright Gray 2012

201 591 9000

A bird's nest; carefully placed and intricately built

CONTENTS

TILLANDSIA USNEOIDES

Old Man's Beard (Air Plant)

GARDENING PASSION

DEDICATION

This work is dedicated to my precious children; Gaile, Patrice, O'Neil and O'Rane

and their spouses, in gracious acknowledgement of their very extensive support.

Also to my grand children Wesley, Shantol, Tevin, Ta'Mal, Ta'Mar, Malik, Anya, Kalya and

A'Drian who love to have their meals on the porch, from where they can get a glimpse of the

beautiful Caribbean Sea. This glimpse often turns out to be the powerful inducement to go

for a swim at the famous Boston beach, Portland, Jamaica.

Boston Beach, Portland, Jamaica

GARDENING PASSION

THE BOOK

Gardening Passion is the creation of a passionate and eloquent manuscript and a floral biography which comprehensively depicts and expounds many intimate gardening encounters while sharing the satisfactory results. Focused around the author's garden, this book speaks of first-hand experiences and is backed by research. The inspirational and authentic photographs are universally understood and play a pivotal role in its creation. The astounding collection was compiled over many years and is attested by the gradual changes depicted in the garden. With the authority and assurance of someone who demonstrates both deep passion and uncommon expertise, the conversant writer takes us chapter by chapter through the life of the garden. She demonstrates a number of creative skills which are also dispersed throughout the book. All of the eight chapters offer activities meant to engage all categories of readers so that they can share the undiluted experiences.

Books are common resource materials, but Gardening Passion is structured in a unique style, giving it a distinct edge. It is poised to penetrate its way into public libraries, learning institutions and into the hands of interior decorators, plant and flower enthusiasts as well as all who pursue gardening knowledge. It includes related subjects such as photography, design art, crafts, interior decorating and party planning in gardens. This complete gardening helpmate is your cordial invitation to a new world; a world that offers fulfilling and rewarding gardening past time, peace, beauty and an intriguing relationship with nature. This "conversation piece" sets no boundaries, no restrictions on age, socio-economic status, gender, or nationality. Everyone will find virtue and value in the countless treasures contained within its pages.

Torch lily

ABOUT THE AUTHOR

The author is a retired educator who for a number of years also indulged and served the general public in the field of commerce. She is currently the President of the Portland Chapter of the Jamaica Horticultural Society. She is a member of the Lay Magistrates' Association of Jamaica serving as a Justice of the Peace for the Parish of Portland. She seeks to uphold her profession, to stretch her range of influence and to disseminate information of much desirability, through writing and photography. She has always loved flowers and is drawn to their captivating beauty, colour and fragrance. She is also a contributor to the Health, Home and Garden Jamaican Magazine.

Her association with flowers dates back to her early childhood, when her mother adorned their dwelling house with freshly cut flowers from the home garden. Her interest began early when aspects of gardening were introduced at school. That programme trained students in areas of Agriculture, Culinary Arts, Leadership and Social Skills, thus preparing and influencing them into productive vocations. It provided a cadre of leaders capable of contributing to national development. The author regards the rich exposure and the positive values learnt then as "Lessons for Life," and has never departed from the concepts. It was under the auspices of the Jamaica Agricultural Society that the 4-H Clubs of Jamaica, a school and community based movement was formed. And so; at about age ten she became the first secretary for her school's 4H club.

Training was not restricted to agricultural activities and gardening techniques. They were also exposed to disciplines that included public speaking, record keeping and fashion designing. It is from this springboard that she landed into gardening. As a youngster her gardening group at school won first prize for the best garden, while she took over the landscaping activities at home. The goal of the 4-H movement was and still is; to mould the head, hands, heart and health of the youngsters, to develop life skills and prepare them to become self-sufficient citizens. She is a testament to the success of the 4-H movement meeting its mandate. Today, the 4-H Club of Jamaica remains the leading youth organization on the island. Now as she continues to participates in 4-H Club activities, she does so with deep sentiments, because she is one of the proud beneficiaries of this holistic movement.

Having established her very own home garden, many years later she ventured to write this very intimate episode. She initially sought not to include anything, be it photographs of flowers, trees or settings that she had not herself encountered. However, as her scope widened she realized that there were many grandiosities around that were ideal for this exotic collection. And so with permission, she utilized her photography skills and included pictures of irresistible, rare plants and lovely settings that she felt compelled to share with everyone.

Upon retirement she enrolled with the Writer's Bureau in the United Kingdom and worked assiduously towards attaining the prestigious status of a published author. The art-oriented author embraced photography and found it easy to arrange and shoot inspiring pictures. Having received home tutorials from a devoted graphic artist, she was able to provide both artistic and design inputs while meticulously compiling her first non-fiction book.

PREFACE

It was a sunny afternoon in spring, when three of my gardening fans stopped by and proceeded to look around the garden. The gleaming sun setting in the far west pitched its light on the trees and formed elongated silhouettes on the green lawn. The annuals and the perennials were in full bloom, the birds were chirping overhead and the fishes were swimming in their quiet pond. As we strolled and as my visitors acclaimed, I teasingly handed them more blooms. Each bloom brought on an elevated level of fascination accompanied by excited outbursts. It was a question innocently posed by one of the ladies that startled me and triggered my desire to write. While standing there in awe and holding by now a bunch of blooms in her well-manicured hands she lovingly raised them to her bulging bosom, tenderly held there and she innocently enquired, "If I plant these, will they grow?"

Months after the encounter I pondered her question. The answer I found, later compelled me to share my experiences in the cultivation of plants and flowers. For years I have been prompted to show my modest collection to the public. With this book, I will be able to defend what has been declared: "It is selfish to keep all this knowledge to oneself." I now seek to disseminate a wealth of information which will bring about a positive change in the lives of many people. Gardening is an awe-inspiring way to communicate with nature and a wonderful escape from the hassle around us. Since then I have set out to write; not a fiction, not a biography, but a textbook with much passion. I wanted to include everything I know about gardening, garden-oriented people, accessories, places of horticultural interest and a wide assortment of gardening activities. I also wanted to include photographs that I had been collecting as a hobby. I envisioned a big book filled with information on plants and their adaptability. I wanted my book to be instructive, mesmerizing and fulfilling. I had no clue though, as to what would be involved in the writing, publication nor the marketing of such a book. At this time, do allow me to ironically say, that it was good that I lacked such knowledge.

I did not own the tools required for modern writing, but I had the tools I knew about; a pen, paper, my dictionary of treasured sentiments and a clipboard. I reached for them, sat under a shade tree in the garden, tilted my head back, closed my eyes and searched keenly around the garden settings. And so, on day one I wrote the outline for the table of contents. Then the scampering through old volumes of newspapers, scrap books, books and magazines began. Countless hours were spent at several libraries skimming through books, though so foreign to the knowledge I sought. I did not miss out on the field trips, the-horticultural shows, garden visits, nature walks and snapping photographs. That became my second nature.

Hibiscus schizopetalus
"Coral Hibiscus"
Split Petal Hibiscus

I discovered later, that a book of this calibre required a team who would apply professional services. I thought that it was now high time to throw in my towel. Patience, however, took hold of me for yet another time. I entered the world of computer graphics and I laboriously applied the graphical skills and techniques I was taught. The offerings of the services I needed to add the professional touch and the superb finish had entered my world. This I regard as a divine intervention and a miracle. It has been nine years since this book has totally consumed my attention. I often felt that I had bitten off a little more than I could chew but there was always a voice that reminded me, that I had reached too far on the journey of achieving my writing goals to turn back. While the challenges were numerous and the anxiety high, my desperation often went undetected. The journey to write this book has been strewed with failures, disappointments and near mishaps. It meant burning the midnight oil, becoming a recluse and making grave self denials. It even meant turning a blind eye on my beloved garden at times.

INTRODUCTION

Gardening Passion is an all-new literary classicism. It is a manifesto for environmentalists everywhere. It has gloriously captured the rhythms of our everyday engagement with the indoor as well as the outdoor spaces. The chapters range from showy plants bearing universal and local identifications, the cultivation of lavish landscapes, favourite trees, to hosting parties in the garden. The book speaks to the creation of elegant gardens, aesthetics in the garden and of various ways to decorate both the interior and exterior of your home using your own plants and flowers. The goal of "Gardening Passion" is to disseminate information at all levels, promote awareness in horticulture, communicate better gardening techniques and encourage amateur gardeners to strive to accomplish beautiful home gardens. Additionally it aims to ensure that the passion for gardening starts growing in all of us.

My hope is that Gardening Passion will heighten awareness of the simplest plant found in your environment and prompt you to treat it with respect and high regard. Evidently, there is an increase in the popularity of plants showcased by plant lovers and a generated interest in Jamaican flora which has been spreading worldwide. This could be attributed to Jamaica's flamboyant and winning participation in the internationally renowned Royal Horticultural Shows held annually in Chelsea, in the United Kingdom.

An early exposure to horticulture fostered an interest in pets as well as wildlife, some of which influenced the plants I selected to cultivate. Hence, the inclusion of photographs of the dreaded but friendly lizard, the soldier crab and the jumping toad. I also included plants that are of sentimental value to me as some were given by friends, some by people who had no particular interest in plants and others by plant enthusiasts whom I have met along the way, and who have become important to me. With much nostalgia, I have included those my mother used to plant, such as the roses, crotons, hibiscus (shoe black) and the morning glory. I also included plants, blooms and fruits trees hat remind me of my past. You may find all your favourites here. These including plants such as orchids, roses, lilies and ornamental trees, which added a new dimension to the garden. I tried to include as many plants as possible, from easy to grow and adaptable, to plants that need extra care and attention as well as some succulents and cactus for tough and sunny areas. Much attention has been given to house plants and other shade-loving plants. I also included experiences of the night time garden, and some advice on how to share and enjoy your garden in general. In my selection of plants I evaluated certain attributes, such as their flowers, fragrance, foliage and fruits. Gardening Passion is comprehensive, easy-to-read and beautifully illustrated to take the guesswork out of gardening. Be cognizant that gardens change with the seasons, so plants, techniques, materials and lifestyle are constantly broadening the choices you have. Gardening Passion provides all the information you need to create lavish landscapes, beautiful gardens and suitable accessories. Additionally you can indulge in related activities; arranging flowers or decorating the interior of your house using supplies from the home garden.

Pause at the welcome chapter. Acquaint yourself with the exhibition, then take a step into a gallery loaded with home-grown plants that are identified by both their botanical and local names. Having left the gallery, timely turn the pages. Indulge in the all-inclusive 646 original photographs. Note the many tested gardening advice, the innovative decorative ideas and the creative displays. See the essential information on gardens, plant care, garden accessories and the therapeutic benefits of gardening. This ground-breaking resource book is an indispensable reference, comprising of 280 pages, illustrated by photographs which are artistically embedded in the manuscript. Gardening Passion is intended for students, horticulturists as well as enthusiasts. However, I am sure that this presentation will appease the curiosity of all audiences. It is both basic enough for the novice and comprehensive enough to help those with more experience improve their gardening habits. Gardening Passion leads all readers down the path to a simpler and more successful gardening adventure.

How To Use This Book

The first pages of the book carry the required formalities of a book of this nature. The preface gives an insight into the development of the book and the introduction opens your appetite for the feast on the pages that follow. Chapter one, which is referred to as a gallery is alphabetically arranged with the botanical and local names of the plants, foliage and blooms included. To ease your acquaintance with new and unfamiliar plants, each entry features information on the general requirements of the plant, such as light, water, humidity and propagation. If you do not find a particular plant here don't be dismayed, as a number of other plants are appropriately dispersed throughout the book.

The comments are meant to answer questions gardeners generally asked about an unfamiliar plant. What is the name of the plant? Where should I plant it? When do I plant it? Will it bloom in the shade? Will it survive drought and neglect? Is it suitable for outdoors or indoors? Can it be grown from seeds? Photo Courtesies are recorded by page number. The back pages include a dictionary that gives the meaning of essential words used throughout the book. The usual bibliography has been omitted to provide more pages of pictures and text.

The index indicates the page on which you will find the information for which you seek. Pictures are placed at strategic points for interest, motivation and identification.

A symmetrical driveway

GARDENING PASSION

ACKNOWLEDGEMENT

Allow me to express my appreciation to all who assisted me with the successful establishment of the garden and ultimately, the compilation of this book. Thanks to a beloved teacher, whose gift of a dictionary I still use and cherish. To Linval Wright, Vincent Barrett, Delroy Pinnock, the gardeners; who over many years continue to toil with me as we establish and maintain the landscape. Many thanks to my co-photographer, Alvin Davis, who often altered his schedule, ran and caught the blooms and settings I got so excited about and to Shantol Smith, my personal photographer, for my portrait and other pictures.

For gifts of plants and garden accessories I say thanks to: Jane Allen, Linnette Anderson, Lola Badresingh, Jeremiah Barckley, Lola Barnett, Desrine Blackett, Christopher Blair, Enid Boothe, Doreen Bramwell, Kay Brown-Cunningham, Ivor Bryan, Wynette Bryan-Joachim, Shirley Buckley, Lillian Byron, Cynthia Campbell, Hyacinth Campbell, Lloyd Campbell, Maureen Campbell, Shaina Campbell, Vadnetta Cassie, Elva Cato, Hopeton Clarke, Joan Clarke, Dukley Clachar, Carol Dallen, Kevin Davis, Shirley Durrant-Irving, Constance Edwards, Lindel Edwards, Alice Ellis, Sammy Ellis, Allison Francis, Damion Francis, Thomas Francis, Steady Frater, Vernon Gay, Glenford and Marlene Gayle, Keith Goldson, Cynthia Hanson, Genevieve Hanson, Allison Hawthorne, Myriel Henry, Adele Horne-Stephens, Patrick Hudson, Glen Ivey, Beverley Jackson, Peter Jackson, Beryl Jengelley, Mamie Kanamori, Hudson King, Vinette Logan, Denise Lewis, Jethro Lynch, Pearl Jones, Lorna Lawrence-Thomas, Juliette Matcham-Sinclair, Elaine Green-McFarlane, Hermine Green, Rohan Lawrence, Verica Merchant, Pauline Miller, Yvonne Morris, Barrington Murray, Bernice Goffe-Murray, Pat Myers, Avis Neufville, Monique Oates, Rosemary Parkinson, Everton Pearce, Verna Prince, Diana Rennocks, Kay Robinson, Vivienne Smart, Noel Smith, Paulette Smith, Delroy Stewart, David Sullivan, Rosa Sutherland, Authur Thaxter, Carmen Watson, Katus Watson, Maureen Weise, Daphney Bingham-Williams, Claudia Williams, Yvonne Williams, Julien Wright, Kenneth Wright and Diana Wynter.

Thanks to graphic artists Jasper Bernard and Miguel Guy. Jasper Bernard has, irrespective of the numerous challenges, conscientiously tutored me throughout the process. I am thankful for the general helpfulness of Mrs. Ann Girvan, Mrs. Veronica Johnson, Miss Carmen Morgan and Mr. Leroy McKenzie for their sharp eyes. To Mrs. Sheryl Horne-Mair, Mrs. Lorna Irving for the editorial services they so competently rendered. Thanks to the individuals and institutions for the comments made on the back cover of the book. I do appreciate the kindness of those named on the photo courtesies page, these pictures have really served to further enrich the photographic aspect of the book.

I thank my children, Gaile, Patrice, O'Neil and O'Rane, and my immediate grandchildren, Wesley, my strong arm, Shantol, my patient and indispensable right hand, Anya and Kalya my young fellow-gardeners; who in their constant desire to express their love, supported wholeheartedly the fulfillment of my gardening "whims and fancies". Thanks to my niece Emancia Neufville for her continuous motivation and to my cousin, Ceceille McQueenie; the graceful model.

I pay fervent tribute to Sheba, who was the family's pet dog, and who, for fifteen years served as my devoted security and gardening companion.

Photo Courtesies

(by page number)

OXALIS TRIANGUARIS
Love Plant, False Shamrock,
Purple Shamrock

STRONGYLODON MACROPODIUM Jade Vine

CHAPTER ONE

A GALLERY OF BEAUTIFUL PLANTS

"What a desolate place would be, a place without

flowers!

It would be a face without a smile, a feast without

a welcome."

Clara L Balfour

This flamboyant gallery is chock-full of treasured and original photographs, exhibiting an interesting array of beautiful plants and blooms. See the lush variegated foliage, intimately combined to appease your floral appetite and to hone your desire to indulge.

Some entries in this chapter are recorded as a collection. All are arranged in alphabetical order using botanical names. The common names of the plants appear in common letters. We find that the naming of plants is generally intimidating, more so, the botanical names. This is a challenge that plant enthusiasts should strive to overcome. It is worth the effort to become familiar, noting that when we shop for plants or attend flower shows and botanical gardens, all the tags or labels carry botanical names. We are aware too, that common names can be notorious and often refer to more than one plant. Not every plant carries a common name.

Entries on Air, Humidity, Water, Repotting and Reproduction attempt to answer questions gardeners generally ask about new plants. Comments and observations are made as a hobbyist and not a botanist. They are meant to add a little more information about the plant: maybe its origin or its culture and to provide a few suggestions on how they can be utilized for your utmost benefit.

If at the end of this chapter you haven't seen your favourite plants, not to worry as a wide range of plants, flowers are scattered in the following seven chapters, find them in the landscapes, in the garden beds and even in the house.

ACALYPHA   Puss Tail

Air Humidity: Moist air.

Light: Semi-shade.

Temperature: Warm.

Propagation: By seeds or cuttings.

Water: Keep compost moist.

Repotting: Repot or prune in spring.

Comments: The Acalypha is a quick growing shrub. There are two groups of Acalypha. The more popular type bears long tassels of tiny flowers and the rich green foliage is plain. The other has colourful, marbled foliage with insignificant blooms. They flourish in humid surroundings. When the air is dry the leaves fall. Take cuttings each year to provide a fresh supply. This shrub is highly regarded as hedge material and as a specimen plant. Remove dead tassels and prune back to half its size in late spring to induce a compact form. Spider mites seem their biggest enemy.

A. wilkesiana

A. wilkesiana

A .Torta

A.   hispida
(Red hot catstail)
(Chenille Plant)

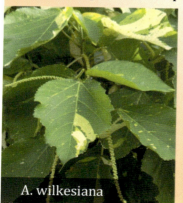

A. wilkesiana

A Llustris

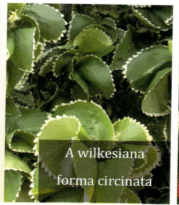

A wilkesiana
forma circinata

2

ADENIUM   Desert Rose

Desert rose

Humidity: No misting necessary.

Light: Full sun.

Temperature: Warm.

Propagation: By seeds or cuttings.

Water: Apply water sparingly during the cool season.

Repotting: Repot in spring every three years.

Comments: The The Adenium or Desert Rose is another attractive flowering plant for the home garden. It was discovered in the tropical and sub-tropical area of the Middle East and Africa. It is a semi-deciduous, succulent shrub or small tree grown outdoors. It makes a fine container specimen. The Desert Rose is prized for its clusters of pink, yellow, red or multicoloured flowers, its tight clusters of narrow, green attractive foliage, thick stems, fleshy branches, dramatically swollen trunk and excellent drought tolerance. It is not demanding and has only a few maintenance requirements; occasional fertilizer, minimal irrigation and occasional pruning.

This distinctive plant features flowering branches that rise from the bottle-shaped caudex (round, fleshy stem base). It has become a first choice for outdoor and more so for rocky landscapes. It is a star of the succulent garden; a beauty of a plant which thrives in hot, dry, sunny conditions. The trumpet-shaped flowers bloom all year. This plant reaches up to 5 feet tall with the lower portion of the trunk swelling to half its height. The sap is poisonous. Propagation is typically done by seeds that should be planted as soon as possible after the pod ripens to maximize the chances of germination. It can also be propagated from branch cuttings, but these plants often fail to develop the characteristic and highly desired bulbous stem. You may also propagate by cleft grafting; this method produces flower within a year.

AGLAONEMA Chinese Evergreen

Humidity: Moist air is necessary.

Light: Semi-shade. Keep away from direct sunlight, the plant will thrive in poorly lit conditions.

Temperature: Warm.

Propagation: Pot shoots with a few leaves and roots attached.

Water: Apply water sparingly during the cool season. Water thoroughly during the rest of the year.

Repotting: Repot in spring every three years. Use a potting mixture of loam, coarse sand and leaf mould. Add compost to which a handful of charcoal has been added.

Comments: The Aglaonema plant family is comprised of over forty species of foliage plants. They make popular house plants, are hardy and do not demand continuous attention. They will accept open ground culture in a shaded spot. They are also pest resistant. These low growing plants require frequent feeding and do not need frequent repotting. The Aglaonema is a favourite potted plant which tolerates both indoor and outdoor conditions. It is an ornamental and decorative plant. Its beauty lies in the large, spear-shaped, plain, striped or dotted leaves mounted on short stems. The flowers are inconspicuous, white or greenish, with spathes that give way to red or yellow berries. The sap is poisonous if ingested and may irritate sensitive skin.

Aglaonema sp. (Silver Spear)

A.commutatum (Silver Queen)

Aglaonema sp.(Teardrops)

Aglaonema sp.

A. violacca (mauve)

A. violacca (chocolate)

A. violacca (yellow)

ALLAMANDA   Golden Trumpet

Air Humidity: Surround the root with damp compost and mist the leaves when you water.

Light: Some direct sun is essential for colouration.

Temperature: Warm.

Propagation: Take stem cuttings and apply rooting horone.

Water: Water moderately.

Repotting: Repot or cut back in spring, yearly.

Comments: The Allamanda was introduced to Jamaica in 1789. It is a forest liana or climber in its wild state. It is now being trained and used as a shrub and is often grown in this fashion in the tropics. The original colour of its flower is yellow, but other colours; mauve and chocolate, have been raised. Allamanda will grow at all altitudes and thrives well in good soil to which a handful of charcoal is added once per year. Ants favour the roots, so keep the bushes pruned and open to avoid infestation. Prune frequently, as younger shoots carry the best blooms. Young plants require a lot of water but older plants are drought-resistant. Start grooming as a shrub specimen, or climber at an early stage to ensure the desired shape. Allamanda enhances the landscape as well as the container; displaying its dark green, leathery foliage and large clusters of rich long-lasting blooms. The sap is poisonous.

ALOCASIA Coco Plant, Chris Plant

Air Humidity: Mist leaves frequently.

Light: Bright light, but avoid direct sunlight.

Temperature: Warm.

Propagation: Divide rhizome at repotting time.

Water: Keep compost moist at all times.

Repotting: Repot annually in early spring.

Comments: The Alocasia is an ornamental foliage plant with a thickened underground stem. Some carry metallic leaves with scalloped edges. They thrive best in a mix of good soil, compost or manure. Leaf mould and builder's sand to which a handful of charcoal has been added will complete the preferred mix. Plant so that a portion of the base is exposed above the surface of the soil. Older parts of the plant may be cut down and the upper portion with foliage may be planted immediately. The underground stem may be cut in 3 in. pieces. Do not water until young buds appear.

The Alocasia is a very sensitive plant that requires ideal conditions. Keep it in the greenhouse or in full shade where it can enjoy the preferred humidity. They relish the shade supplied by shade trees; where they produce enormously large, spectacular leaves. Once there is a sign of ill-health, remove all the leaves but the newest. Repot in new soil and water sparingly. The leaves of the Alocasia Black Magic become black in full sun, while it is very happy growing in water.

A. sanderiana

A. amazonica

A. eminens
A. Black Magic)

A argyrea

ALOE VERA Sinkle Bible

Air Humidity: No misting necessary.

Light: Sunny spot.

Temperature: Warm.

Propagation: By removing and planting offsets.

Water: Once per month during summer.

Repotting: Every 2-3 years.

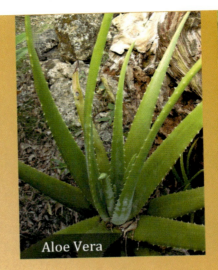
Aloe Vera

Aloe Vera blooms

Comments: There are over 250 species of Aloes in the world, mostly native to Africa. It is a member of the Lily family. The Aloe Vera s a semi tropical succulent plant and has long been a popular houseplant. It is often called the 'miracle plant' or the 'natural healer'. This succulent is one of nature's perfectly packaged miracles and is also known as the Miracle plant. Cut the fleshy leaf and observe how the plant quickly seals in the vital juices. The cut section will heal over the end where it was sliced and retains its plumpness to remain green for several days. The medicinal sap has been used to soothe the pain associated with burns, rashes, insect bites and other skin irritations by just removing a lower leaf from the plant, slice it open and apply the gel on the affected area. This herb is widely used in cosmetics. The sap of the Aloe is a thick, mucilaginous gel. It is this gel which is used medicinally. The sap has a bitter taste and may even be unpleasant in the raw state. The addition of some fruit juice helps to make it more palatable.

Older specimens may bloom, producing a tall stock covered with bright coloured coral flowers. The nectar from the flowers is a favourite food for hummingbirds. They should be planted in full sun or light shade. The soil should be moderately fertile and fast draining. Established plants will survive a drought quite well, but for the benefit of the plant, water should be provided.

GARDENING PASSION

ALPINA Red Ginger, Ginger Lily

Air Humidity: Mist leaves occasionally.

Light: Bright light, some shade.

Temperature: Warm.

Propagation: By dividing the rhizomes.

Water: Keep compost moist.

Comments: Alpinia purpurata, known also as Ostrich Plume and Cone Ginger, is a tropical flowering plant that grows to 6 ft. in height and produces a 12 in. tall flower, with long, brightly coloured red, pink or white bracts. The bracts look like the blooms but the true flower is the small white flower. Gingers are a large and varied clan with diverse flower forms, exotic colour combinations and scented blossoms.   It prefers partial shade and moist humid conditions, although it can tolerate full sun in some climates. It likes to be well watered and not left to dry out.

A.purpurata
(Red Ginger)

Ginger can also be grown as a houseplant and its cut flowers can be used in floral arrangements. Plant them in a location where the soil drains well. You may amend the soil with the addition of organic material to raise the level 2-3ins. to improve the drainage. Plant your ginger rhizome with any roots pointing downwards and the "eyes" or growing points just below the soil surface. Press the soil down to remove any air pockets. After planting, water your ginger generously. Water periodically during the growing season. Gingers appreciate a monthly feeding of any balanced (10-10-10) fertilizer. Cut back the ginger lilies to the ground after they bloom. Ginger lily is resistant to most pests and diseases.

ANTHURIUM Flamingo Plant, Oil cloth, Tail Flower

Air Humidity: Mist leaves frequently.

Light: Protect from direct sunlight.

Temperature: Average warmth.

Propagation: Divide the rhizome at repotting time. Plant in coir, rotted wood, sea almond husks, compost or coconut husks. As the roots reach out of the container, turn them back in. Keep the roots covered but not stifled.

Crystal Anthurium

Water: Apply a little water every 3-4 days.

Repotting: Repot in spring every 2 years.

Comments: There are two groups of Anthurium; the "flowering" and the "non-flowering." The flowering type is noted for its brightly coloured, leathery bloom; while the non-flowering is prized for the remarkable beauty of its foliage. The blooms last for many weeks and they bloom all year round. We sometimes call the spathe a flower, however, this is really a modified leaf. The spathe may be multi-coloured or carry a single colour of red, white, yellow, mauve, pink or burgundy. Feed flowering Anthurium with a few grains of osmocote every 2 months to enhance blooming. **The Crystal Anthurium** (Anthurium crystallinum) displays very unusual foliage. The young leaf changes from bronze to purple, to deep green. The foliage hangs vertically and shows off the prominent silvery veins. Repot every 2 years. To propagate, cut off the portion of root that is hidden under the surface. Cut this in 2-3 in. pieces. Plant and wait for the new shoots. When these are big enough, separate them. Each shoot represents a new plant.

Anthurium blooms

A young leaf, and a bloom of a hybrid Anthurium

APHELANDRA   Zebra Plant

Air Humidity: Mist leaves frequently.

Light: Partial shade, as colours fade in bright light.

Temperature: Average warmth.

Propagation: Take stem cuttings in spring.

Water: Keep compost moist.

Repotting: Repot in spring every 2 years.

A. squarrosa

Comments: Aphelandra squarrosa, known as Zebrsa plant, makes a wonderful zebra houseplant. The intriguing foliage and the production of the beautiful bracts is your reward for the care you give your plant. The blooms and the corrugated striped leaves, serve as a double-purpose plant. These leaves grow to about 9 ins. long and a few inches wide within the centre of the leaf and they have pointed tips.

All year round its croton-like, shining, emerald, elliptic leaves with silvery veins provide attractive foliage. In the autumn it is crowned with long-lasting, bright yellow or orange flowers. There are species with orange or scarlet blooms and grey-veined leaves. Zebra plants like slightly higher humidity than many other plants. You may need to raise the humidity levels in a room artificially by placing the plant in a humidity tray with pebbles. With pruning, regular feeding and moist compost it will not become leggy. It is handsome in large pots and elegant as a specimen plant. When the flowers begin to die remove them. Prune the stem and leaves so there is only two rows of leaves in height left. This will help prevent the plant getting leggy and losing leaves and will give the plant an opportunity to grow the following year. Propagate new plants from the cuttings.

ASPARAGUS Fern

Asparagus Fern

Air Humidity: Mist leaves frequently.

Light: Partial shade.

Temperature: Average warmth.

Propagation: Take stem cuttings in spring.

Water: Keep compost moist.

Repotting: Repot in spring every 2 years.

Comments: The Asparagus Fern is native to Southern Africa and is grown as an ornamental plant. It is not a true fern and its leaves are really needle-like branches. It is much easier to grow than true ferns. It is found in the garden, in containers as a house plant and in hanging baskets. It is used to decorate the deck or patio and helps to clean indoor air. The attractive foliage is also used in floral arrangements. It is very hardy and adapts readily to cultivation. It will adapt to variations of lights, does not demand a humid atmosphere and can be easily propagated.

When growing asparagus ferns outside, place them in a shady location for best foliage growth. Under ideal conditions the plant will sometimes flower, followed by berries. Berries can be planted to propagate the asparagus fern plant. The tiny white flowers are small and not necessary for the beauty of growing asparagus fern. The frilly, feathery asparagus fern plant is easy to grow. Note that they have thorny spurs so one should wear gloves during asparagus fern care.

AZADIRACHTA INDICA A JUSS

Neem

The Neem tree is popularly known as "the tree of the 21st century." It is one of the most promising of all plants and is poised to benefit everyone.

Neem

The Neem is described as "nature's gift to mankind", the "tree for many occasions"," the tree that purifies", " the wonder tree", "a tree for solving global problems". Azadirachta indica, means the "free or noble tree of India," suggesting that it is intrinsically free from pests and diseases and is benign to the environment. It is a member of the Meliaceae family and is botanically a cousin of the mahogany tree. It is a tall, spreading evergreen tree, bearing small, shining, bitter-tasting leaves and small white flowers that are highly aromatic. No other plant yields as many strange and varied products and has as many exploitable by-products as the Neem. This tree is known to have over forty uses and is widely used in the agricultural sector. It is known to provide millions with inexpensive medicines.

BEGONIAS

Air Humidity: Moist air.

Light: A brightly lit spot away from direct sunlight. The morning sun is highly beneficial.

Temperature: Average warmth.

Propagation: Propagate with new shoots or from leaf cuttings.

Repotting: Seldom needs repotting

Water: Water freely but do not keep compost soggy.

Comments: Begonias are grown for their display of rich dark foliage and hefty, gorgeous blooms. They provide splashes of unusual dark bunchy colours for indoor as well as for outdoor. All Begonias detest over watering and direct sun. The most common types are the fibrous rooted or wax begonias and the tuberous begonias.

B coccinea

B. masoniana
(Iron Cross)

B. feastil bunchil

B. grandis

B. pizzazz pink

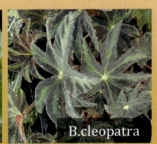
B.cleopatra

B.schmidtiana

B. blucerna

B. pizzazz

Tuberous begonias grow best in partial shade. They need light portions of fertilizer, as excess cause flower buds to drop. Begonias will adapt to full sun or partial shade and those with bronze foliage do better in the sun than the green varieties. Wax Begonias withstand drought and heat better than their counterparts.

BOUGAINVILLEA   Paper Flower

Pink Bougainvilla

Air Humidity: The rains will provide enough moisture.

Light: Plant in the sunniest, driest spot available.

Temperature: Keep warm.

Propagation: Take cuttings from ripened wood in spring or summer.

Water: Will tolerate the driest conditions, water during the hot months.

Repotting: Seldom needs repotting, cut back instead.

Comments: The Bougainvillea is a vigorous, woody climber; blooming in big panicles of reds, plum purple, pinkish yellow, yellow, white or pink. Then there is the marvel of the trio of colours, borne by a single plant, known as "Surprise" or "Conversation Bougainvillea". It is the favourite of dry tropical gardens. It can be trained to climb trellises or be planted as an attractive but thorny barrier. It is easy to be trained as a Bonsai, due to their ease of training and their radiant flowering during the spring. It makes as a colourful groundcover for large areas.

Bougainvillea will grow well in any type of soil. Once your bougainvillea is established, it should thrive with very little care other than the pruning. If planted in a pot you may need to fertilize. Choose a fertilizer with calcium nitrate. During the spring and summer, fertilize your plant every-other week. During the cooler months fertilizing it once every four to six weeks. Bougainvillea is a relatively pest-free plants. It makes an excellent hot season, drought tolerance plant in the landscape. The sap of the Bougainvillea can cause skin rashes.

BROMELIADS Bromelia

Tillandsia cyanea
(Blue -Flowered Torch)

Bromeliads
sunburst

Tillandsia (Flowering
Pineapple, not edible)

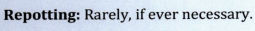

Earth Star
(Starfisf plant)

Air Humidity: Mist leaves during summer.

Light: Most Bromeliads require a brightly lit spot, away from direct sunlight. Pineapples and Earth Stars will thrive in full sun.

Temperature: High temperature is required to bring plants into flower, but average warmth is satisfactory for foliage types.

Propagation: Offsets appear at the base of the "mother" plant. When the offsets are several months old, remove them with some roots attached and plant in shallow container. Discard the old plant as it will not flower again.

Water: Never over water. Provide good drainage. Keep the central 'vase' filled with water. Wet the compost when it dries out. With non-vase varieties, keep the compost moist but never wet.

Repotting: Rarely, if ever necessary.

Comments: Feeding through the funnel formed by the leaves is the natural method of nutrition. Some Bromeliads are grown for the beauty of their foliage while others for the grandeur of their bold flower heads. This plant can be described as a rosette, with leathery, strap like foliage. The flower pops up on a stalk from the vase or the centre of the rosette. This bloom often lasts for several weeks.

Earth Stars These are found in a wide range of interesting colours, tones of stripes and banded in green, red, brown and yellow. The leaves are succulent with wavy margins and teeth-like edges. The white flowers appear nestled in the centre. New plants called "pups" grow out on the side of the plant and are easily removed to start a new galaxy of Earth Stars.

Anasas comosus

GARDENING PASSION

BRUNFELSIA   Yesterday- Today -And -Tomorrow

Air Humidity: Mist leaves during the hot summer.

Light: Bright sunlight.

Temperature: Warm to cool.

Propagation: Take stem cuttings in spring or summer. To propagate, cover 6 in. long cuttings with a clear plastic bag, place this in semi-shade and keep in humid conditions. It will take as much as 6 weeks for the new plant to show. Remove plastic bag and water the new plants.

Water: Water regularly.

Repotting: Best in spring.

Brunfelsia calycina

Brunfelsia sp.

Comments: The beautiful flowers of Yesterday-Today-and-Tomorrow go through an interesting metamorphosis that has earned it its common name. The rounded, 3 in. blooms open as a deep violet blue. Within a day the colour changes to pale violet. By the third day the colour fades again to nearly white and on the fourth day it dies. It takes several days for the flowers to go through their complete colour changes, while they emit a lingering sweet, sugary, candy-like fragrance. A prolific bloomer, it produces flowers almost non-stop all year long. Even fallen flowers retain their sweet fragrance. The fragrant blooms are attractive to bees, birds and butterflies. The seeds and all other parts of the plant are poisonous if ingested. Like most other plants, pinching off the growing tips will encourage bushy growth. Feel free to pinch any time of the year. Old branches should be pruned to half the previous growth. This plant can be successfully grown in pots.

CACTI Prickle Plant

Air Humidity: No misting necessary.

Light: Choose the sunniest spot. Some shading may be necessary in the hottest months.

Temperature: Average warmth.

Rebutia minicula
(Mexican Sunball)

Heliocereus speciosus
(Prickly Pencil)

Rubella senilis

Propagation: Cuttings of most varieties root easily. Take stem cuttings or offsets in spring or summer. It is vital to let the cuttings dry for a few days (large cuttings for 1-2 weeks) before planting.

Water: Increase watering in spring. Water thoroughly when the compost begins to dry out. Use tepid water. In late summer give less water and after mid autumn keep plant almost dry, just enough water to prevent shriveling.

Repotting: Repot annually or when necessary. Transfer into a pot which is only slightly larger than the previous one.

Comments: The Cacti are a distinct group of succulents. There are two types of Cacti, the **Desert type** and the **Forest type**. They originated in the dry areas of the world, so their preference is sandy, free draining compost, sunshine, fresh air and some water. Cacti are indeed easy to care for and can withstand a great deal of neglect. They are cultivated for their weird appearance, or for their surprisingly beautiful blooms.

O. opuntia, (Irish mittens)

CALADIUM, Elephant Ears, Angel Wings

Humidity: Mist leaves frequently, especially during spring and summer.

Light: Well lit spot but away from direct sunlight.

Temperature: Warm.

Fertilizer: Feed monthly with a light foliage fertilizer.

Water: Water freely during the growing season.

Propagate: From tubers in early spring.

Repotting: Repot in spring.

Comments: Caladiums are tender, foliage annuals, grown for their spectacular, multicoloured, decorative leaves. The leaves are paper-thin, beautifully designed and heart-shaped. Like other annuals they are not permanent and last only from spring to early autumn.

Mass them together and create a focal point in the landscape, as they provide a striking contrast with the green lawns. Plant them in pots, in borders and shaded areas. At the end of the season, allow the soil to dry, dig the tubers out and set them in a warm place to dry. Replant in early spring. Store the potted ones in a dry place until spring.

C. candidum

C. Rose Glow

C. hortulanum sp.

C. Thai beauty

C. Freda Temple

C. hortulanum sp.

C. Red Flash

C. Polka Dot

C. White Star

C. Pink Beauty

CASUARINA EQUISETIOLIA Willow

Willow

Air Humidity: Mist leaves, if potted.

Light: As much light as possible.

Temperature: Cool temperature.

Propagation: From seeds or cuttings.

Water: Seldom.

Repotting: In spring

Comments: The willow is a lofty, fast growing ornamental tree. The leaves are in fact needle-like branches. Willow cuttings root easily because the tissues contain a natural root-promoting hormone. They root readily from cuttings or where broken branches lie on the ground. To start a tree from a cutting, select a healthy branch that is approximately 1/2 in. -1 in. in diameter and about 10-15 in. long. Plant into moist soil leaving two or three leaf nodes above ground. Roots will start to form within a few weeks. You can also use the layering technique. Simply take a stem, nick the stem with a knife and then bury the wound under soil while the stem is still attached to the tree. After 6-8 weeks you can cut the stem from the mother plant and dig up the cutting with new roots attached.

The jagged seeds are light and easily blown around in the wind. Willow roots spread widely and are very aggressive in seeking out moisture. Willow thrives in salty soils hence, their presence on the seacoast. To prune and shape the tree can result in the plants becoming debilitated and susceptible to insects and fungus. It has been noted that some of humans' earliest manufactured items such as fishing nets, baskets and wattle fences were made from willow. Willows produce a small amount of nectar hence its attraction to bees. The charcoal we use in art class, for drawing, is made from the willow. Living sculptures are created from live willow rods planted in the ground and woven into shapes such as domes and tunnels, known as Topiary.

CELOSIA Cock's Comb, Plume Flower

C. cristata

Air Humidity: Mist leaves occasionally.

Light: Bright light.

Temperature: Warm.

Propagation: Sow seeds.

Water: Keep compost moist.

Comments: The Cock's Comb is a hardy, showy, quick growing annual. It is extensively cultivated in China. It thrives well in alkaline soil and enjoys lots of water in dry weather. Cocks comb flowers are seen in vibrant yellows, pinks, reds and gold colours, there is no fragrance.

There are two types, the Celosia plumosa with feathery plumes and the Celosia cristata with a curious, velvety bloom that resembles the cock's comb. There are about 60 species of Celosia. The contorted floral heads of the crested type of Cocks comb continue to enlarge throughout the growing season. Perched on long stiff stems,

Celosia plumosa make excellent fresh floral arrangements and will last from 5-14 days of vase life. They are also beautiful in dried flowers arrangements. Prune or cut regularly to obtain robust blooms. Plant in beds or in pots and enjoy the heavily clustered or slim-line blooms that last for many weeks. Space plants 8-12 in. apart. They grow best when mulched. Spray the foliage with a dilute solution of liquid fertilizer to give them a boost.

C.plumosa

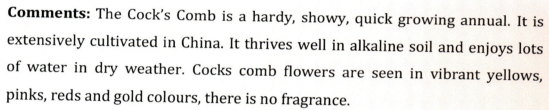

20

COCCOLOBA Sea Grapes

Air Humidity: No misting necessary.

Light: Full sun.

Temperature: Warm.

Propagation: Use a rooting hormone.

Water: Water generously during the dry season.

Repotting: Repot in spring.

C. uvifera

Comments: Sea grapes grow wild in the tropical climate and are mainly found along the sea coast. The plant consists of stiff, rounded, olive-green leaves. The very broad leaves are between 8-12 in. When immature, the foliage is red in colour and as they age, change colour until they are green and laced with red veins. In time, fragrant white or ivory flowers appear, followed by clusters of green, grape-like fruits that turn purple when ripe. The juicy, sour-sweet, marble-size fruits are edible. As a child I consumed so many sea grapes. We also made jams and refreshing grape juice. The grapes will thrive in fertile, well-drained soil. Older plants are able to survive high temperatures but young plants are likely to die.

Sea grapes are propagated naturally by their seed. This method does not give you any control over the gender. Only female plants produce fruit but, the male plant must be nearby for her to produce. Taking a cutting from an existing plant may obtain a more predictable result than that obtained from seedlings. Water the plant daily until well-established. Prune sea grape regularly to maintain its shape and remove dead branches. Use them as wind breakers, hedges or as attractive specimen plants. Plant grape plants along boulevards and highways.

COCOS NUCIFERA Coconut Tree

Everybody knows the coconut palm. They are the universal symbol of the tropics and are grown around the world in lowland, tropical and subtropical habitats. The two main types of coconut palm trees are known as "talls" and "dwarfs." Talls are the most common type with variations such as Green and golden Malayan and May Pan. Tall coconut palm trees are cross-pollinated and produce a high yield, while dwarf coconut palm trees are self-pollinated, making them genetically homogeneous.

Coconut palm

The coconut palm produces small yellow blooms with a sweet scent and taste. Male and female flowers are borne on the same plant. The pollination happens by wind and flowers grown on a 3-6 ft. long branched inflorescence eventually matures into coconuts. The palm tree comprises of a trunk and a bole. Its round base is called the "bole". The trunk is the upper section of the tree.

It is self-cleaning; dropping its old branches at intervals thus making it very easy to maintain. The spineless branches are yellow-green and are about 15-17 ft. long, with 2 ft. long leaves symmetrically grown on each side of the branch. Each coconut palm tree has between 2,000-4,000 roots that can grow as deep as 16 ft. Unlike most other plants, the palm tree has neither tap roots nor root hairs, but has a fibrous root system that is strong enough to anchor the tall tree during any storm. Palms are becoming a more dominant feature in the landscape. So if you are looking for a tropical feel, then the palm is exactly what you need. It has been successfully used as a background tree, a framing tree and as a specimen plant.

CODIAEUM Crotons

Croton sp.

Air Humidity: Mist leaves during the hot season.

Light: Bright sunlight.

Temperature: Warm.

Propagation: Take cuttings in spring and use a rooting hormone.

Water: Water generously, especially in the dry season.

Repotting: Repot if necessary.

Comments: Crotons, Codiaeum variegatum, are tropical shrubs with highly ornamental leaves, artistically coloured in bands of red, burgundy, yellow, dark green, mauve, orange and almost black. They show their brightest colours when grown in direct sunlight for at least 6-8 hours a day. Most have laurel- like foliage but there are those with forked leaves, lobed, long ribbons, twisted and curled leaves. They grow to a height of 6 - 8 ft and width of 3 - 6 ft. They are attractive as a single plant or a group and grow well in pots or in the ground. You can grow cultivars of crotons such as "Norma," "Petra," "Banana," "Bravo," "Gold Dust," "Ice-tone Red," "Karen," "Mammy" and "Sunny Star" in the warm outdoors.

Well-drained soil works best for growing crotons outdoors. Pots should provide good drainage. Crotons prefer humid weather. Mist the plants throughout the hottest days of summer to help the leaves stay bright and healthy. Outdoor crotons require weak applications of fertilizer. Too much fertilizer can damage the roots and cause the leaves to be dull. Crotons are generally pest-free, but may be affected by mealybugs and thrips. Treat pests with a pesticide developed for tropical plants. They grow into massive bushes so prune to maintain a shrub-like appearance. They make gorgeous driveway décor and are used as a "quick fix".

A COLOURFUL ASSORTMENT OF CROTONS

C. Bravo

C. Petra

C. Eburneum

Croton sp.

Croton sp.

C. variegatum (Craigii)

C. punctatum ureum

C. Variegatum "Gloriosum"

Croton sp.

Croton sp.

C. Golden Ring

C. Aucubifolium

C. variegatum (Norma)

Croton sp.

Croton sp.

COLEUS Joseph Coat

C. Trailing Salamander

C. Solar Sunrise

Air Humidity: Moist air.

Light: As much light as possible.

Temperature: Average warmth.

Propagation: Take stem cuttings in spring or summer.

Water: Keep compost moist at all times.

Repotting: Cut back and repot in spring.

Comments: Joseph Coat, also known as Poor Man's croton, surpasses its stately rival in the brightness and colour range of its foliage. They may not be as imposing as the long-lasting crotons but they make fine multicoloured displays. They are easy to grow and are equally pleasurable to care for. This soft-stemmed plant needs pinching out regularly to stop the plant becoming leggy and defoliated. By pinching, you will lose those not- so- significant blooms but the plant will be bushier and will last longer.

Treat this plant as an annual and set new plants each spring. It is fun to collect and grow the many available colours. Plant them in beds and organize them to form numbers or letters as they are utterly breathtaking in mass plantings. Arrange them in geometric shapes.

C. Kong Red | C. Electric Lime | C. sp | C. Wizard Jade | C. Pistachio Nightmare
C. Wizard Mosaic | C. Oxblood | C. Red Head | C. Flame Nettle | C. sp.

COSTUS Spiral Ginger

C sp. (Crepe ginger)

Air Humidity: Best when placed on a gravel tray or grown near a water source.

Light: Bright indirect sunlight.

Temperature: Keep plants shaded.

Propagation: Propagate by dividing the thick, ginger-like rhizome.

Repotting: Repot in spring.

Water: Keep roots moist at all times.

Costus sp.
(Indian –head ginger)

Comments: Costus is a group of perennial herbaceous plants. It is widely found in the tropical and subtropical regions. Costus is a large genus containing 90 species. It is often characterized and distinguished from relatives such as <u>Zingiber</u> (true ginger) by its spiralling stems. The genus as a whole is called spiral gingers. As the name implies its foliage spirals around bamboo like stalks.

Some varieties have a velvety soft texture on the back of its leaves. Others are smooth with purple undersides. Its bracts and flowers range from a cone like bract, pineapple shaped or soft crepe like flowers emerging from green cones. It is very easy to grow. They do well in partial sun. Plant them in rich well draining soil kept moist. They make beautiful garden specimens or container plants for the garden or patio. Costus dubius, is known by the common name Spiral flag, which describes the twisted or spiral arrangement of the leaves on the stems of this species. The open flowers contain nectar and attract a range of pollinators.

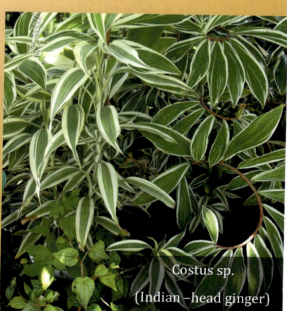

Costus sp.
(Indian –head ginger)

DELONIX REGIA

Poinciana Tree

The Poinciana, known by many names; Flamboyante, Peacock Flower, Flame of the Forest, is a member of the massive legume family. It is a flowering tree noted for its fern-like leaves and flamboyant display of red, orange or yellow flowers. The bright green compound leaves have a feathery appearance and are doubly pinnate. Each leaf is 30–50 cm long, has 20-40 pairs of primary leaflets and each of these is further divided into 10-20 pairs of secondary leaflets. The Poinciana requires a tropical climate and can tolerate drought and salty conditions. The Poinciana's size works well as a shade tree along avenues, in parks and large gardens. It is very widely grown in the Caribbean more so, in St Lucia. Many Puerto Rican paintings feature these flamboyant trees.

The Poinciana is the national flower of St. Kitts and Nevis. I was flabbergasted when a flight I was on, touched down in St. Lucia and I saw an island looking like a massive garden overgrown with the flamboyant Poinciana. The Poinciana is definitely the most popular flowering shade tree in the Caribbean. It is revered as an ornamental tree. In June through to September, the Poinciana puts on a riotous show of its voluminous clusters of bright coloured blooms.

DIEFFENBACHIA Dumb Cane

D. Amoena sp. (Tropic Snow)

Air Humidity: Mist frequently.

Light: Partial shade, bright light, some morning sun.

Temperature: Average or above average warmth.

Propagation: Cut off and pot the crown of the plant. Pieces of stems, 2 or 3 in. long can be used as cane cuttings. Some varieties produce "daughter" plants at the base which can be removed and used as cuttings.

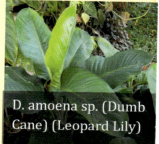

D. amoena sp. (Dumb Cane) (Leopard Lily)

Water: Water regularly.

Repotting: Repot in spring every year.

Comments: Dieffenbachia is one of the most spectacular group of house plants. The plant is grown for its large, variegated, leafy foliage. They make a widespread greenhouse favourite but flourish in any cool, shaded outdoor location. They are hardy and will withstand the indoors well. They respond well to hot or cool temperature. They need some sun to keep the plant from becoming top heavy. Some of the older leaves will fall and give the plant a False Palm effect. When this happens you can cut the crown off and use this as a new cutting.

D. picta Camilla

As the plants age it may be necessary to support them as they tend to become leggy and even unattractive. These plants are also called "dumb canes" because eating them would irritate the throat and vocal cords. They are considered poisonous to humans and animals if eaten. Cut cane down to visually appealing level or cut out the new growth. A healthy plant will soon put out new growth where it has been topped out. Old leaves will fall off to make way for new ones.

D.picta Exotica

D. bausel

DRACAENA

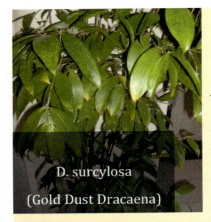

D. surcylosa
(Gold Dust Dracaena)

D.godseffiana
(Gold Dust Dracaena)

D.massangeana
(Corn Palm)

Air Humidity: Mist leaves regularly.

Light: Light shade is best, but some varieties must have good light.
Temperature: Average warmth, some species can withstand lower temperature.

Propagation: Remove crown from old, leggy canes and plant in rich soil. Pieces of stem 2 or 3 in. long can be used as cane cuttings.

Water: Keep compost moist at all times.

Repotting: Repot in spring every 2 years.

Comments: The leafless, woody trunk and crown of beautiful foliage is the characteristic of the Dracaena group of plants. This gives them a distinct Palm-like appearance, but they are not at all related to the Palms. Not all Dracaenas are Palm-like. The D. godseffiana and D. surcylosa are shrubs which bear no resemblance to their relatives. The D. marginata and D. draco are two easy species to grow and are in high demand as house plants. Their popularity as plants for interior decorating is due particularly to their tolerance of low light levels. Some species are grown as Ti Plant. Grow your own Ti Plant by planting a piece of mature cane cut from Dracaena, Cordyline or Yucca.

Some species and varieties of Cordyline are often confused with Dracaena. The difference is that **Dracaena** has a deep yellow or orange, non- creeping rootstock, while the **Cordyline** has a white and knobby, creeping rootstock.

DRACAENA

D. sanderiana

D. drementis (Janet Craig)

D.marginata tri-colour

D. Dragon Tree

D. demensis warneckii

D. sanderiana (Lucky Bamboo)

CORDYLINE

C. terminalis (Fruiticosa)

C. terminalis (Ti Plant) (Red Dragon) (Red Dracaena)

C. terminalis (Tri Colour) (Red edge)

EICHHORNIA CRASSIPES Water Hyacinth

Water Hyacinth

Air Humidity: No misting necessary.

Light: As much light as possible.

Temperature: Cool temperature.

Propagation: Divide young shoots.

Water: Ensure that the water does not dry out of the container.

Repotting: Repot yearly.

Comments: The Water Hyacinth was introduced from South America. It is an aquatic, ornamental, free-floating perennial plant that can grow to a height of 3 ft. The leaves are 6–8 in. across and float above the water surface. The shiny leaves are light to dark green and circular to elliptical in shape. They have long, spongy and bulbous stalks. An erect stalk supports a single spike of 8-15 with conspicuously attractive lavender to pink flowers with peacock-like markings located on a terminal spike.

Underneath the water is a thick, heavily branched, dark, purple-black fibrous root system. These roots trail underwater in a dense mat that covers the entire surface of the pond. The roots spread rapidly in freshwater and will kill fish and any other aquatic animal so they should be controlled. By shading the water, these plants deprived native aquatic plants of sunlight and animals of oxygenated water. Water Hyacinth grow best in still or slow-moving water. Each plant can produce thousands of seeds each year. The seeds are dispersed by birds. These seeds can remain viable for more than 28 years.

EPISCIA   Flame Violet

Air Humidity: Mist leaves infrequently.

Light: Brightly lit, but shaded spot.

Temperature: Average warmth.

Propagation: Take runners in spring.

Water: Keep compost moist.

Repotting: Repot every 2 years.

E.cupreata
(Flame Violet)

Comments: The Episcia or Russian Violet is an attractive trailing plant which is not as popular as its well known relative; the African Violet. Episcia is a genus of about 8 species and are found in the tropics. The species are perennial herbaceous. They are primarily grown for their showy metallic-like leaves that grow in a rosette and reach 2-3 in. long. They combine shades of green and coppery brown, with light green or silver veins. They bloom pink, red, yellow or white bell-shaped flowers all year round.

E.cupreata
(Carpet plant)

The most luxuriant blooms are produced under greenhouse conditions as they requires high humidity. They are really difficult to grow in a hanging basket. Instead they are most comfortable on the ground between taller plants where they can benefit from the increased humidity. The runners root in surrounding compost. Repot in spring every couple years to refresh the soil. Flame violet has shallow roots and a spreading habit, so a wide, shallow pot works best.

FERNS

Air Humidity: Moist air.

Light: Bright indirect light.

Temperature: Average warmth.

Propagation: From spores or from rhizomes. If it produces rhizomes, divide the plant into 2 or 3 pieces in early spring. Some ferns produce young plants at the ends of runners.

Water: Keep compost moist.

Repotting: Repot in spring when the roots fill the pot. Most plants will probably require annual repotting. Do not bury the crown of the plant. Prepare suitable soil and add compost.

Platycerium bifurcatum
(Staghorn Fern)

Comments: Ferns are rosettes of divided arching leaves which are referred to as fronds. Some ferns have spear-shaped leaves and button-like leaflets. Many ferns are ideal for hanging baskets, others are large enough to be displayed on their own, while others are tiny and delicate. Generally, ferns are categorized as Maiden Hair ferns, Walking ferns, Rabbit's Foot ferns, Baby's Breath and Bird's Nest ferns. Despite popular opinion, ferns are not shade nor indoors lovers, as most varieties originated in the dappled brightness of tropical woodland. While many of the ferns can be drought tolerant, once established, most ferns benefit from supplementary watering. Ferns prefer to be left alone to multiply and do not like to be divided on a regular basis. Groom the ferns by removing all dead and damaged fronds so that new ones can develop.

ASSORTED FERNS

Pteris dretica albolineata (Variegated Table Fern)

Phyllitis scolopendrium umdulatum (Hart's Tongue Fern)

Pellaea rotundifolia (Button Fern)

Platycerium grande (Elkhorn Fern)

Polypodium ureum (Hare's Foot Fern)

Nephrolepis exaltata bostoniensis (Boston Fern)

Asplenium nidus (Bird's Nest fern)

Adiantum raddianum (Maidenhair Fern)

Nephrolepis exaltata Gloriosa (Ruffles)

FICUS   Fig, Rubber Plant

F.elastica robusta

Air Humidity: Mist leaves occasionally in summer. Misting is essential for the trailing types.

Light: Bright spot for tree types, partially shaded spot for others. The Rubber Plant will adapt to sunshine, but too much sun can be fatal to the creeping type.

Temperature: Average warmth.

Propagation: Take stem cuttings and use a rooting hormone. Air layer the woody varieties.

Water: The tree types prefer to have the compost dried out to some extent between watering. The trailing types require more frequent watering.

F.benjamina starlight

Repotting: Avoid frequent repotting, do so every 2 - 3 years.

Comments: This is a huge tree family, growing up to 60 ft. tall and 60-70 ft. wide. It is a hardy evergreen as well as a deciduous plant. The powerful roots of the trees run for great distance and are capable of boring through cement and road surfaces. The dense rounded canopy and gracefully drooping branches of the ficus makes it quite popular as a landscape tree. Thick, shiny, 2-5 in. long, evergreen leaves, generously clothe the long branches. Dense branches will weep towards the ground, so dense that nothing grows beneath it. The Rubber Plant heads this powerful family. It is easier to grow than its variegated family members. This makes it a splendid specimen plant for the home or office space. The variegated ones, as well as the green ones are commonly used for fencing. The ficus is ideal when trained as a Bonsai or crafted as a Topiary.

F. benjamina variegata

F. elastica decora

FITTONIA

F. argyroneura nana
(Snakeskin Plant)

Air Humidity: Moist air is essential. Place pot on a pebble tray or mist leaves frequently.

Light: Choose a partially shaded spot and avoid direct sunlight.

Temperature: Average warmth.

Propagation: Creeping stems will root in surrounding compost, remove and pot the rooted cuttings.

Water: Water liberally from spring to autumn.

Repotting: Repot in spring. Keep the plant shaded.

Comments: The Fittonia is a novel, low-growing creeper, with fleshy, trailing stems and brightly coloured oval leaves. It is grown for its heavily veined, ornamental foliage. It produces some insignificant spikes white or cream in colour.

F. verschaffeltil
(Net Leaf)

These should be pinched off since they are unattractive and utilize the plant's energy which is better devoted to the development of its intricate foliage. The Fittonia grows about 6 in. high, with an indefinite spread. The leaves bear a network of white, pink or red veins. This pattern is responsible for all the common names; Net Plant, Lace Leaf and Snake Plant. Fittonia likes a good soil mixture consisting of a generous amount of sand, rich loam soil and leaf mould. The tendency of the inadequate root system is to rise out of the growing medium. Address this by the occasionally dressing with a mixture of sand and manure. Any straggly growth should be cut back in the spring. The Fittonia is susceptible to mites, snails and slugs. Be prepared to ward them off.

GERBERA   Gerbers

Air Humidity: Mist leaves occasionally.

Light: Well lit, but away from direct sunlight, they benefit from afternoon shade.

Temperature: Average warmth.

Fertilizer: Fertilize with a bloom booster, once every 2 weeks for maximum blooms. Apply a time- release fertilizer every 6 to 8 weeks.

Water: Keep compost moist. Water regularly during the blooming season .

G.jamesonii Happipot

(African daisy)

Repotting: Discard old plants and plant young shoots.

Comments: Gerbera, like Orchids, enhance modern living. Gerbera is a large genus in the same family as sunflowers. They are native to South Africa. They were initially bred to be cut flowers and are still the 5th most common cut flower in the world. The blooms are in single or double form and come in red, yellow, orange, bronze, pink and white. They appear between May and August. The extra tall flower stalks give the plant a lanky appearance and cause the blooms to bow to the ground. New and more compact strains have been developed with shorter stalks. The crown sinks in the soil after 2 years, so plant in new beds every two years. Ensure that the crown is not covered; the point where the stem meet the root, is slightly above the ground level. Covering the crown will cause the plant to suffocate and rot. Gerbers are susceptible to crown rot, so don't plant them too deeply. They are also susceptible to powdery mildew, so avoid overhead watering. Water the plants early in the day, giving the foliage a chance to dry out before night fall, thereby discouraging fungal diseases.

GLORIOSA Glory Lily, Climbing Lily

Air Humidity: Mist leaves occasionally.

Light: Indirect sunlight.

Temperature: Average warmth.

Propagation: From seeds and tubers.

Fertilizer: Fertilize once every month.

Water: Water liberally, keep the vine moist.

Repotting: Plant tubers or cut offsets in spring.

G. rothschildiana

Comments: Gloriosa is a genus of 12 species. They are native of tropical and southern Africa. The many common names are flame lily, fire lily, gloriosa lily, superb lily and creeping lily. You will be required to erect a strong trellis 6- 8-ft. before planting this vine. Select a location that receives 6-8 hours of direct sunlight but at the same time will keep the roots shaded. Prepare the soil and amend it with generous amounts of organic matter or well-rotted manure. Plant the tuber in a 6 in. pot in an upright position, with the tip 1 in. below the surface. Transplant when the plant has six leaves.

Plant your Gloriosa lily in the spring. Place the tubers approximately 3 - 4 in. from the trellis. Dig a hole, 2 - 4 in. deep and lay the tuber on its side in the hole. Cover the tubers and gently firm the soil. Look out for the large, long lasting, colourful flowers on 4 ft. slender stems in mid-summer. The unusual twirl-like petals are red, with a yellow base. The stems are weak so provide support for them. Water sparingly at first, but be a little more generous as the plant begins to grow.

GRAPHTOPHYLLUM Match-Me-Not, Fresh Cut

Air Humidity: Mist leaves frequently.

Light: Semi shade or full sun.

Temperature: Warm.

Propagation: Take stem cuttings in spring.

Water: Water thoroughly and regularly.

Repotting: Repot in spring.

G. pictum chocolate

Comments: There are many varieties of this woody, evergreen shrub, which are grown for their brightly coloured, oval shaped leaves mounted on upright stems. The waxy leaves carry a soft sheen. The mature plants, at 2 years, produce an influx of ruby or purple flowers in late spring and summer. Crush or pound the leaves and extract the juice which is believed to heal skin wounds, hence the name; Fresh Cut.

G pictum-var mentha

Match-Me-Not works well in containers, in hedges and as a foliage accent. Assorted colours work well when planted in the same container or in the same hedge. Plant in any good soil with good drainage. Plant in full sun to partial shade for best leaf colour. There is no need to fertilize. Pinch growing tips and prune to shape.

G. pictum Eldora

G pictum, alba variegata

G. pictum caricature

G.pictum (Tri colour)

HELIANTHUS ANNUUS   Sun Flower

Air Humidity: No misting necessary.

Light: Plant in as much light as possible, or in full sun.

Temperature: Warm.

Propagation: Propagate from the multitude of seeds.

Water: Keep the rich soil moist at all times.

Repotting: Repotting is not necessary.

Comments: The Sun Flower is a hardy, quick growing annual. It can grow up to 8 ft. high and produces large 8–12 in. yellow blooms. What is intriguing about the Sun Flower is that at sunrise its face is turned towards the east. However, over the course of the day, it moves to track the sun from east to west. During the night, it returns to an eastward orientation. The wild Sun Flower which blooms a variety of colours, typically does not turn toward the sun but may face many directions when mature. Sunflowers are so easy to grow. The seeds are edible and are used as food for birds.

HELOCONIA Wild Plantain

Humidity: Mist during the dry season.

Light: Plant in as much light as possible.

Temperature: Warm to cool.

Propagation: Divide rhizome in spring.

Water: Keep the rich soil moist.

Repotting: Repot in spring.

Heliconia sp.

Heliconia sp.

Comments: The Heliconia, a very colourful flowering shrub that is closely related to the Banana and to the Strelitzia. Observe the leaves to see the relationship to the banana and observe the blooms to see the resemblance to the Strelitzia. In spring they produce pendants bearing 1-2 ft. long flower-heads often called "lobster claws." Those that are variegated produce better foliage under partial shade. Flower stalk and leaves should be cut to ground level when bracts fade.

HIBISCUS   Shoe Black

H. rosa-sinensis

Air Humidity: Mist leaves occasionally.

Light: Full sun.

Temperature: Warm.

Propagation: Root cuttings together. Treat cuttings with rooting powder.

Water: Keep compost moist at all times.

Repotting: Repot in spring.

Comments: The Hibiscus is a handsome, tropical, evergreen shrub and is one of the most widely grown plants in the Caribbean. The blooms are single, double or triple, and last for 1 or 2 days. With proper care there will be a succession of blooms all year round. They thrive at any elevation, grow in any well-drained soil and prefer full exposure to sunlight. Prune often, as younger shoots are more floriferous. Fertilize once per year and add some home-made compost three times yearly. Some species can be difficult to grow. The short life span of the blooms does not allow for insect pollination. One plant can be made to accommodate two or more colours. Do this by grafting on to the mother plant. The varied coloured blooms are much employed by decorators. Look out for the enemies; the ants, snails, scale insects and mealy bugs.

Hibiscus sp.

Hibiscus sp.

Hibiscus sp.

Hibiscus sp.

HIBISCUS SYRIACUS Rose of Sharon

Air Humidity: No misting necessary.

Light: Full sun.

Temperature: Warm.

Propagation: From stem cuttings or air layering.

Water: Keep the soil moist.

Repotting: Repotting may not be necessary, but best done in spring.

Comments: Rose of Sharon is a shrub. Pruning can create a simple main trunk; thus it is often referred to as the Rose of Sharon "tree." Prune accordingly during its first two seasons. It can also be groomed as an espalier, that is, to be grown over a flat trellis. The distinctive characteristic of the double petal Rose of Sharon is that, its white bloom becomes light pink after midday then turns to a darker shade of pink in the afternoon.

It prefers rich, loose and well-drained soil. Older plants may fall prey to fungal damage if grown in areas without full sun. Use it in landscapes as the attractive and plentiful blooms make this outstanding plant fully capable of holding its own as a focal point or as a specimen plant. The Rose of Sharon is a prime candidate for effective hedges. This bush is deciduous and can be used to achieve privacy around sections of the garden. The Rose of Sharon blooms single or double petals profusely from June through to September. The blooms can attract too many bees. It belongs to the Hibiscus family and offers colours when many shrubs have long ceased blooming.

The single petal experiences no colour change

At 9.30. A M (EST)

At 1.30.P M(EST)

At 5.15 P M (EST)

HYDRANGEA Mop Head, Hortensia

H. macrophylia

Air Humidity: Mist leaves occasionally.

Light: Bright light, away from direct sunlight.

Temperature: Prefers cool and humid conditions.

Propagation: Root cuttings together and place in a moist place.

Water: Water well in hot weather, using rainwater.

Repotting: Repot in spring.

Comments: Hydrangea is unique in its colour formation; the pink Hydrangea becomes blue as the flower gets older. Add extra sand to the loamy soil to assist with drainage, since Hydrangeas are sensitive to clogged soil. Plant in rich soil; from which lime is absent. Prune often by cutting out spent shoots. Blooms are produced from young, second year wood growth. Cut mature blooms, dry these and enhance your dried floral arrangements.

IMPATIENS Busy Lizzy

Impatiens

Air Humidity: Mist leaves.

Light: Bright light, but avoid direct sunlight.

Temperature: Average warmth.

Propagation: Stem cuttings or seeds.

Water: Keep compost moist.

Repotting: Repot in spring. The pot must be filled with roots before the plant will flower freely.

Comments: Its name is a strong indication of its non-stop blooming habit. The stems are transparent, fleshy and carry oval -shaped leaves. The plant bears blooms in single or double petals, with plain or variegated foliage. The seeds of some species hang in little pockets and at your touch will burst open and disperse the seeds; hence another pet name 'Jump up and kiss me'. Impatiens are easy to grow, but require regular care. Pinch out the tips and prune back mature plants. Support the stems.

IXORA

Air Humidity: Prefers airy surroundings.

Light: Full sunshine.

Temperature: Warm.

Propagation: Use cuttings and apply a rooting hormone.

Water: Keep compost moist.

Repotting: Repot in spring.

Comments: The Ixora is also known as the Flame of the Woods. This large, tropical flowering shrub branches freely, is a prolific bloomer and makes a popular hedge material and specimen plant. Once established the lustrous clusters of red, yellow, salmon, pink and white will continue throughout the year. Ixora looks quite stunning when grown beside the wall of the house or allowed to pose beside a column. The blooms are ideal for fresh floral arrangements.

I. undulata

I. coccinea (Compacta)

Chinese ixora

KALANCHOE PLANT   Velvet Plant, Leaf of Life

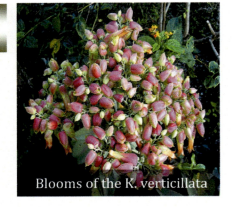
Blooms of the K. verticillata

K. verticillata (Tree of life)

K. beharensis (Velvet Plant)

Kalanchoe sp.

Air Humidity: No misting.

Light: Full sun to partial shade.

Temperature: Warm.

Propagation: From stem or leaf cuttings or by small offsets at the base or on leaves. Set leaf cuttings in sand.

Water: Seldom needs watering.

Repotting: Repot every two to three years.

Comments: There are many varieties of the Kalanchoe plant which are grown for their unusual leaves or for their interesting blooms. There are two basic types, the K. blossfeldiana and the Velvet plant; the more popular and the K. marginii hybrids or Leaf of Life. The Velvet plants are pretty large in stature and, under the right conditions they reach 12 ft. in height. The large opposite leaves are triangular and irregularly lobed.

The Leaf of Life are grown for its showy salmon and yellow blooms. The blooms appear in many shapes, forms and colours and usually last for many weeks. Prune severely after blooming. There is no need to fertilize. The nature of the Leaf of Life, suggests the freedom with which the plant grows as there are plantlets which grow along the leaves margins or tips. Over-watering is the most common cause of plant failure. Kalanchoe is very easy to cultivate and makes an ideal addition for the rock garden.

LAGERSTROEMIA   June Rose

L flos-reginae

Air Humidity: Mist leaves.

Light: Full sun

Temperature: Average warmth.

Propagation: Take cuttings in spring.

Water: Water regularly especially in dry weather.

Repotting: Repot in spring; best planted in the ground.

Comments: In May to June look out for crinkled petals in clusters of mauve, pink or white at the end of woody, slender branches. See the peak of blooms in June; hence the popular name June Rose. Prune shrubs annually, preferably in August to within 2 in. of the soil. Add manure and mulch in February.

LANTANA

Air Humidity: Mist leaves occasionally.

Light: Supply as much light as possible.

Temperature: Average warmth.

Propagation: Sow seeds or take cuttings.

Water: Water regularly, provide additional water during dry periods.

Repotting: Repot, if necessary, in spring.

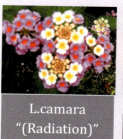

L.camara "(Radiation)"

L. camara " (Mutabilis)"

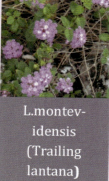

L.montev-idensis (Trailing lantana)

Comments: The Lantana is a free blooming, tropical shrub with coarse leaves and slightly prickly stems. The foliage smells like citrus. It is known for its clusters of small, bright-coloured flowers in yellow, orange, white, red or purple. Cut back in spring and set new plants every 2 years. Lantana is salt and drought tolerant. The Trailing Lantana may be used in hanging baskets. or as ground cover.

LILIUM   Lilies

Empress lily

Air Humidity: Mist leaves during the dry season.

Light: Bright light, away from direct mid-day sun.

Temperature: Cool.

Water: Keep compost moist at all times, especially during the growing period. Reduce watering after flowering as leaves will turn yellow and die.

Propagate: From bulbs stored from previous season.

Comments: Most lilies are referred to as Easter lilies, as it is at that time of the year that they generally bloom. The trumpet, bowl or cap shaped blooms last for 1 or 2 days only, but one bunch may continue to bloom for a number of days. They produce blooms in a rainbow of colours such as red, hot pink, yellow, cream and white and some are heavily scented. The clusters are grown on erect stems that grow from a bulb.

Lilies are perennials and are perfect for potting or planting in beds. They are also beautiful when planted in borders. Lilies carry a special charm and are very pretty when several types are planted in one bed. Lilies make great cut flowers. They are beautiful when mixed with ferns. Plant them away from windy areas as they can become top-heavy when in bloom. Give your lilies a monthly supply of liquid fertilizer. Keep them cool.

Haemanthus ultiflorus
(*Fireball Lily*)

Hippeastrum puniceum
(*Barbados lily*)

Crinum erubescens

Lily sp.

MANGIFERA INDICA Mango

If you love mangoes as much as I do, then your landscape tree planting activities will be incomplete without a mango tree. The mango is known as the "King of Fruits". It is referred to as the comfort food because the fruits contain an enzyme with stomach soothing properties. The sweetest and best flavoured fruits have yellow, red or orange tinges when ripe, and produce flavours that can be described as exotic blends of pineapple and peach.

Mangoes have been cultivated by man for over 4000 years. They are an excellent source of Vitamins A and C, as well as Potassium. They are high in fiber and make a good staple for the daily diet.

Mango tree

They grow best in the tropics as they require hot dry periods to set and produce a good crop. There over 400 varieties of mangoes, many of which ripen in the summer. The most popular varieties are the Tommy Atkins, Haden, East Indian, Bombay, St. Julian (Julie) and common mangoes.

A native to southern Asia, the fruit has been cultivated in many tropical regions and distributed globally. Mango is one of the most extensively exploited fruits as it is used for food, flavour, fragrance and colour. The fruit takes 3-6 months to ripen. Mangoes are ready to eat when slightly soft to the touch. The birds will indicate when the fruits are beginning to ripen and you may need to jostle with them as they too seem to love mangoes. Mangoes can be picked green and left to ripen at room temperature. The mango tree makes a handsome landscape specimen and shade tree. The trees will grow up to 60 ft. tall but can be trained to fit the landscape. The roots are not destructive as they are deep-rooted rather than spreading. Mango trees will grow in any well-drained soil but avoid planting them in heavy, wet soils. Some trees are known to be over 100 years old and are still fruiting.

MARANTA GROUP

Prayer Plant, Peacock Flower

Air Humidity: Mist leaves regularly.

Light: Partial shade, no direct sunlight.

Temperature: Average warmth.

Propagation: Divide plants at repotting time and keep the plants warm.

Water: Keep compost moist.

Repotting: Repot in spring every 2 years.

Comments: The Maranta Group embraces four closely related members: Maranta, Calathea, Stromante and Ctenanthe. One outstanding feature is their spectacular foliage, bearing prominent blotches, stripes and coloured veins. Unlike many plants they should not be allowed to dry out between watering, especially when the plant is growing. If the air is too dry, the tips of the leaves will get dry and the lower leaves may fall. Curled, spotted or yellow leaves are caused by under watering. Do not allow water to stand on the crown. **The Prayer Plant** has a strange habit of folding and raising its leaves at nights. **The Peacock** is peculiar, the leaves die down during the rest period. During this time leave the plant undisturbed. Do not fertilize but keep the compost damp. As velvety, soft leaves appear, look out for small four-petal blooms that will grace the shade garden for many months. The Marantha group makes excellent pot and greenhouse subjects.

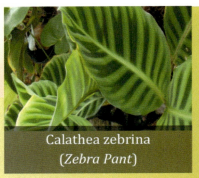

Calathea zebrina
(*Zebra Pant*)

Maranta leuconeura erchoveana
(*Prayer Plant*)

Calathea *makoyana*
(*Peacock Plant*)
(*Cathedral*)

Calathea ornata

Maranta arundinacea
(*Arrow root*)

MONSTERA Split Leaf Philodendron

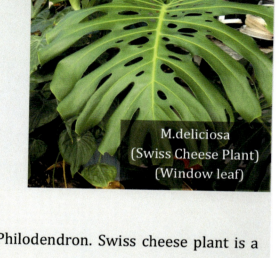

M.deliciosa
(Swiss Cheese Plant)
(Window leaf)

Air Humidity: Mist leaves.

Light: Keep out of direct sunlight.

Temperature: Average warmth.

Propagation: Remove tip at a point below an aerial

and plant the cutting, the parent plant will continue to grow.

Water: Allow compost to dry before watering.

Repotting: Transfer to a larger pot every 2 years.

Comments: Monstera deliciosa has often been mistaken as a Philodendron. Swiss cheese plant is a tropical jungle plant that requires rich soil that holds moisture, yet does not remain soggy. They thrive equally well in most home interiors. As house plant they may require staking. The plants are thick stemmed vines that support themselves on nearby vegetation and produce long roots from the stem to supplement that support. Push aerial roots down in the compost.

With care, giant leaves with perforated and deeply cut lobes will be produced. Holes in the leaves is an added attraction to this plant. A lack of holes in the mature leaves is due to the failure of water and food to reach the uppermost leaves. Leaves with brown papery tips and edges suggest that the air is too dry. A pot-bound plant will show similar symptoms. The plant stops growing altogether if placed in deep shade. Swiss cheese plant may get too big for its container. The plant is known in its habitat to reach 10 ft. tall or more. In the home environment, it may grow too tall, but the plant responds well to trimming. Wash and polish mature leaves. Watch for spider mite infestations. This glossy foliage plant has a long life span and with care will reward you with its enchanting lacy leaves for years.

MUSSAENDA

Air Humidity: No misting necessary.

Light: Full sun.

Temperature: Warm.

Propagation: Treat cuttings with rooting hormone.

Water: Water regularly.

Repotting: Repot after 4 or 5 years.

Comments: Mussaendas belong to the Rubiacea family which also includes the Gardenia, Ixora, Pentas and coffee plants (Coffea arabica). There are over 200 species of Mussaenda with a broad distribution from West Africa. It is is a dramatic, tropical shrub and rambler, which may be shaped as a small shrub or grown in a container. It may also be cultivated as a large tree-like form in the landscape and can grow up trees to heights of 30 ft. It carries hairy, medium-green leaves and prefers full sun. The prolific show of blooms start in spring and last through summer. The plant's colour is produced from the large showy petals which are in fact enlarged floral sepals. These surround the yellow, cream or white flowers. The starry true flowers carry 5 petals and have a crepe like texture. Plants flower from November to May and can flower almost all year round in ideal climates. They provide quite a show in gardens. You can see their bright, gleaming colours from a distance.

M. afrondosa

M. sp. (Peach)

M.sp.(Orange)

M. erythrophylia (Ashanti blood)

Dendrobium or Cane Orchid

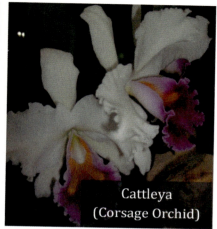

Cattleya
(Corsage Orchid)

Air Humidity: Mist plants twice weekly.

Light: Good light. Some orchids are sun-lovers and need 4 -12 hours of sun each day, while others must be shaded from direct sunlight.

Temperature: Individual types vary. The general rule is a day temperature of about 70°F.

Propagation: Divide plants at repotting time. Leave at least 3 shoots on each division.

Water: Keep compost moist, using soft, tepid water. With Cattleya and Dendrobium, allow the surface to dry between watering.

Repotting: Potting mix ranges from pebbles, moss, tree fern bark, charcoal to coconut fibre. The most important factors are that the medium must have the ability to retain moisture, must not break down too quickly and should last enough time without becoming toxic. Terete and Semi-Terete Vanda require potting in soil. Some orchids thrive better on wooden blocks or in wooden baskets. The medium should be packed firmly, but loose enough to allow root penetration. Pot orchids in shallow, perforated, earthenware pots. They appreciate being pot bound but after a few years repotting and division may be necessary. They welcome a weekly portion of liquid fertilizer. Repot only when growth begins to suffer. Place epiphytic orchids on trees as they constitute attractive landscaping.

PALMS

Air Humidity: Mist leaves.

Light: Palms love sunshine but potted ones are best in partial shade.

Temperature: Average warmth.

Propagation: From seeds which will take up to 3 months before they grow.

Water: Its first need is for good drainage.

Repotting: Only repot when the plant is thoroughly pot- bound.

Comments: Palms are attractive and make a very distinct statement. Some are even known to have a cast-iron constitution. They are tall and stately, with a smooth grey trunk. Some are even swollen above the base and are graced by a heavy crown of arching pinnate leaves. They belong in the tropics, hence the presence of over three hundred varieties with a wide range of leaf point is at its tip. If this is cut the plant will die.

(Bottle Palm)

(not to be confused with the Traveller's palm)

(Sago Palm)
(Cycads) Not a true palm

Caryota mitis
(Fishtail Palm)
(Caryotas urens)

AN ASSORTMENT OF PALMS

Washington shire Palm

Traveler's Palm

Japanese Palm

Palm sp.

Royal Palm

Areca Palm

Bamboo Palm

Coconut Palm

Fan palm

GARDENING PASSION

PENTAS FLOWERS Egyptian Star Cluster

P. lanceolate

Air Humidity: Mist leaves occasionally.

Light: A bright sunny spot. Pentas that do not receive enough sunlight will stretch and become leggy.

Temperature: Average warmth.

Propagation: Take cuttings in spring.

Water: Keep the compost moist.

Repotting: Repot in spring.

Comments: Pentas are semi-tropical shrubs grown as annuals. They grow in clusters in white, red, pink and purple shades. Bees love these nectar-rich flowers and butterflies are attracted to them too. When planted together multicolours are cultivated as cross pollination occurs resulting in an increased colour range. Penta plants may stay in bloom continuously under ideal growing conditions.

The dark green foliage of penta plants is slightly fuzzy. The five-petalled blossoms grow in 3-in. clusters similar to lantana. Pentas need regular irrigation but can tolerate dry conditions. Avoid overhead watering to prevent brown spots on the foliage. They strive best in rich, well-drained soil. Prune the plants to 6 in. in January, when bloom production is at its lowest. Fertilize pentas once a month with a balanced flower fertilizer during periods of active growth. The plant can become straggly, correct this by cutting the blooms, pruning and by pinching out the tips regularly. They thrive in containers and look cheerful when planted alongside other annuals, like zinnias and marigolds. Whiteflies may plague plants grown indoor.

PEPEROMIA

Air Humidity: Mist leaves occasionally in summer.

Light: A bright or semi-shady spot.

Temperature: Average warmth.

Propagation: Cuttings which root easily.

Water: The compost must dry out to some extent between watering.

Repotting: Every 2-3 years.

P. prosrata
(Creeping Peperomia)

P. argyreia
(Watermelon Peperomia)

Comments: Peperomia is a delightful, easy-to-grow houseplant that's been around for years. It is an easy indoor plant quite a small houseplants that does not need a lot of space. Peperomias are compact and slow growing plants with an erect or creeping habit. The patterned leaves are leathery. They prefer a partially shaded, cool and airy location.They can tolerate low light, but do not grow as well and their foliage may not be as interesting They do not require a constantly moist atmosphere and will grow in some degree of sunlight. They like rich soil, coarse sand and manure. Avoid wetting the foliage, as it injures the minute flowers. Turn pots weekly to encourage a symmetrical shape. Fertilize monthly. Water peperomia when the soil. You do not need to worry about fertilizing or pruning them.

P. hederaefolia
(Ivy Peperomia)

PHILODENDRON

Air Humidity: Keep the surroundings moist.

Light: Keep out of direct sunlight.

Temperature: Average warmth.

Propagation: Take stem cuttings from the older stems.

Water: Keep the compost moist.

Repotting: Transfer to a larger pot in spring every 2-3 years.

Comments: Philodendrons are among the most popular, tolerant and durable of all plant families. There are many different species, each possessing its own characteristics of leaf size, shape and colour. Some species climb, while others remain in more of a shrub shape. What they all have in common is their ability to survive adverse conditions. Feed in spring and again in mid summer with a liquid fertilizer. Wash the leaves regularly to prevent the pores from becoming plugged with dust. They grow best when their roots are slightly cramped. Add a moss stake or other types of support to the climbing plant at the time of repotting since some types of Philodendrons produce aerial roots which will cling to whatever support they find. These roots should not be cut off completely, but can be trimmed back.

P. melanochrysum
(Black creeper)

P. billotige

P selloum (Lacy Tree)

P. Sp.(Red merald)

P. Swiss Cheese

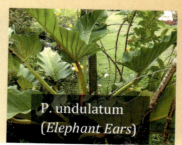

P. undulatum
(*Elephant Ears*)

PISTIA STRATIOTES Water Lettuce

P. stratiotes

Air Humidity: No misting necessary.

Light: As much light as possible.

Temperature: Cool temperature.

Propagation: Remove and plant young shoots.

Water: Its rooting system must be fully immersed in water.

Repotting: Repot when foliage becomes tight.

Comments: Water Lettuce is a free-floating rosette plant with many spongy, dusty green leaves. The bright green leaves are deeply veined and resemble heads of floating lettuce. they grow to lengths of up to 10 in. and up to 4 in. wide. The velvet leaves are covered with very fine hair and are arranged in a spiral pattern from the centre of the plant. The leaves are 1–6 in. wide. The leaves make an enticing place for frogs to hang out. The single species it comprises, Pistia stratiotes, is known as water cabbage, water lettuce, Nile cabbage or shellflower. It was first discovered from the river Nile. It can now be found in nearly all tropical and subtropical fresh waterways. Water Lettuce helps to provide shade for the pond and fish They help oxygenate and clarify the water and reduce the growth of algae. Water Lettuce seems to prefer some shade.

The small, green flowers are seldom seen because they are hidden between the leaves. The root system is very much the same as the Water Hyacinth. Plant in mesh containers that are designed for water gardens as this helps to control the rampant root system. In the water garden they easily propagate and need to be thinned frequently. They are reproduced by seed and by "mother" plants growing "daughter" plants that are attached to each other. They even make for great table top water garden plants or centre piece displays.

PLUMBAGO

P. auriculata

Air Humidity: Mist during the hot season.

Light: As much sun as possible.

Temperature: Average warmth.

Propagation: Seeds or cuttings.

Water: Keep compost moist.

Repotting: Repot in spring.

Comments: The Plumbago auriculata, is known as the Cape plumbago or sky flower. It is a shrub and can grow 6 -10 ft. tall with a spread of 8 -10 ft. It is native to South Africa, This vigorous climber, when trained and supported can be kept as a specimen plant. It can be trained to trail or to climb. Cut back old shoots in early spring. Wait for a continuous cluster of white or blue flowers set among light green leaves to appear throughout summer to autumn.

P. alba

Look out for the tiny seeds and sew them in spring. It can also be propagated from cuttings. It prefers light, well drained soil. Blue plumbago prefers slightly acidic soil. It requires 6-8 hours of direct sunlight, here it will produce much more blooms. The blooms of white or blue are very soothing to the eyes.The deep blue form, 'Royal Cape' does not sucker. You can grow blue and white plumbago together for a mix look or opt for separate colour plantings.

PEDILANTHUS TITHYMALOIDES   Devil's backbone, Monkey fiddle

P. tithymaloides

Air Humidity: No misting necessary.

Light: Bright sunlight.

Temperature: Warm.

Propagation: From stem cuttings.

Water: Water infrequently.

Repotting: Cut stem and pot in spring.

Comments: Pedilanthus   tithymaloides is known as Devil's backbone, Zig-zag plant or Jacob's ladder. This clump-forming succulent shrub will grow to 6ft. tall and to 3ft. wide. It is a succulent and is a distant relative of the well-known Christmas Poinsettia. It carries ovate to elliptic, medium green leaves up to 5 in. long. The bloom is a showy, two-lipped, red bracts encase insignificant tiny . Flowers are clustered at the branch ends and appear in late spring or early summer. Fruits are small capsules. The Monkey fiddle exude a poisonous milky sap when cut. 'Variegatus' has leaves with pink or white variegation. The flowers are described as shaped like slippers, red birds or ducks. This "slipper flower" belongs to the Euphorbiaceous family. These are seen in two varieties; the all green and the variegated. The variegated form takes on a pinkish shade.

These are lovely in pots, in the rock gardens and they make a fine companion for hard and dusty areas. It is very easy to grow. It needs some protection from hot summer sun, but it will be happiest in full sun. Do not over-water as this can cause rotting. Liquid fertilizer may be used once a month. Plant in well drained sandy mixture. The sap is moderately caustic.

PSEUDOBOMBAX ELLIPTICUM

Shaving Brush (Pompom)

Shaving Brush is known as one of the most beautiful, single flower in the world as it makes a magnificent flowering tree when in bloom. It is a succulent, with deciduous characteristics. Its sturdy branches are close to the base of the tree. This spectacular ornamental tree which is a native of Mexico is capable of growing to a height of 70 ft. It makes an excellent spreading shade tree.

Plant this "showstopper bloomer" in your landscape and you too will find that passers-by fully engage their cameras to

Shaving Brush Tree

capture its beauty. The bloom is an eye-catching, thick bush of silky rose pink stamen, topped with yellow pollen hence the name "shaving brush." The fragrant bloom lasts for one day and is magnificently attractive to bees, butterflies and birds. It makes a wonderful conversational tree, excellent quality firewood and the wood is an ideal material for carving handicrafts. It is extremely drought tolerant, but if watered in the summer will grow very fast and is much more likely to flower profusely. Beautiful flowers develop from long cylindrical buds that open with a slightly explosive sound. The open blossoms attract the honey bees. They seem to be entirely interested not in the nectar at the base of the many long stamens but in the pollen at the tips of the stamens.

RHOEO   Moses in the Basket

Rhoeo sp.

Air Humidity: Mist leaves occasionally.

Light: Bright light.

Temperature: Warm to cool.

Propagation: Remove and plant the offspring.

Water: Keep soil moist.

Comments: The Rhoeo ,"Tricolour" gets its distinct name from its lance-like, three-toned leaves, which feature purple undersides with hues of light pink, white and green on top. The leaves are held upright so both the deep green tops and rich purple undersides are visible. Rhoeo has outstanding ornamental features. Rhoeo is known by a number of names such as Moses in the bulrushes, Moses in the boat, Boat lily and Oyster plant. It makes an excellent and fast growing groundcover and lends itself to pots and hanging baskets. This plant is one of the houseplants that needs regular water to look fantastic. Moses in the basket is perfect for desks and table tops. Display them in the kitchens, bedrooms and bathrooms. Look for those small, white flowers tucked into purple bracts.

Water the Rhoeo once per week. Water slowly and deeply down through to the roots. Feed with a general-use fertilizer in the spring. They do not need pruning except to remove faded leaves. Plant them outdoors in garden beds, as borders and in containers. Grow them in shade or semi-shade. They look excellent on their own or as companion for begonias, impatiens and other shade lovers. They withstand drought very well. Caterpillars and mites may attack your plant. Fungus, root rot and leaf spot can all be problems if it receives too much water.

Rhoeo sp.

GARDENING PASSION

SAINTPAULIA   African Violet

S. sp. (white)

S. rupicola
(Frilly Breezy Bue)

Air Humidity: High humidity is essential. Place the pot on a pebble tray or surround the pot with damp mulch.

Light: Bright, but not direct sunlight.

Temperature: Average warmth.

Propagation: Take leaf cuttings.

Water: Maintain proper drainage. Do not wet the leaves.

Repotting: Repot in spring.

Comments: The African violets are purple flowers with a tiny fleck of yellow in the centre. They are native to Africa. Plant them in shallow pots, as the thread-like aqueous root system is not deep rooted. Use a good growing medium. A potting medium suitable for African Violets should be sterilized, and light and airy to allow root penetration.

All varieties have five basic needs; steady warmth, high air humidity, good light, careful watering and regular feeding. Water mainly from the bottom. If water gets on the leaves, dry with a paper towel to prevent leaf spotting. Once a month, plants should be watered from the top to flush out accumulated fertilizer salts. Never allow plants to stand in water. Most violets die from over-watering. The soil should be kept evenly moist and never allowed to become soggy. Water only when the top of the soil is dry to the touch. Keep the plant clean and free of dry foliage and spent flowers. Remove the side shoots. No portion of the leaf should be in contact with the soil as this can cause the leaf to rot. Diseases mainly result from over-watering and inadequate drainage. Increase your stock by setting mature leaves in clean sand, coir or light rich soil.

SANSEVIERIA Mother-in-law's Tongue

S. golden hahnil
(Golden Bird's Nest)

S. hahnil

Air Humidity: No misting necessary.

Light: Requires some direct sunlight .

Temperature: Average warmth.

Propagation: Off springs and leaf cuttings.

Water: Water moderately from spring to autumn.

Repotting: Rarely required.

Comments: The Snake Plant and the Mother-in-Law's Tongue are architectural plants with stiff, upright leaves up to 3 or 4 ft. tall. The Snake Plant has green banded leaves, while the Mother-in-Law's Tongue features a yellow border. These plants are among the toughest of all houseplants. They can withstand any conditions, from dark to bright. The only way to surely kill them is to overwater or never water at all.

The patterned foliage stands erect, fleshy and sword-like, and some species are cross-banded with distinct golden edges. It is a common sight everywhere in Jamaica. Feel free to combine them with other foliage. Under the right conditions sprays of small highly fragrant flowers will appear. The low growing rosette varieties make a fine ground cover or desk accent.

Sweet-smelling blooms

S. trifasciata
(Snake Plant)

S. trifasciata laurentil
(Mother-in-Law's Tongue)

SCINDAPSUS Creepers, Devil's Ivy, Pothos

S. aureus (Devil's Ivy)

Air Humidity: Mist leaves frequently.

Light: Well-lit, sunless spot, variegation will fade in poor light.

Temperature: Average warmth.

Propagation: Take stem or root cuttings. Keep compost rather dry and leave in the dark until rooted.

Water: Water liberally from spring to autumn. Let compost dry out slightly between watering.

Repotting: Repot, if necessary, in spring or summer.

Comments: Creepers are best known for their shining, marbled, heart-shaped leaves. They are classified in the group of best used house plants. The marbled features of the variety of creepers makes them excellent plants for indoor use and are used in a number of ways by interior decorators. Creepers are used as ground cover, as a focal point in hanging baskets and as a desk accent. One of the primary reasons creepers continue in popularity is that they can tolerate lower light, lower humidity and cooler temperatures than many other plants. They also function well as air cleaners. Creepers will also thrive in water only and do equally well in moist soil. Wash and polish leaves to bring out the fine beauty. Prune to promote new growth.

Pothos pictus
(Elephant ears)

S. aureus
(Marble Queen)

SPATHYPHYLLUM   Peace Lily

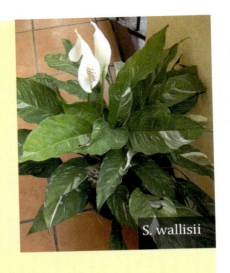

S. wallisii

Air Humidity: Mist leaves regularly.

Light: As much light as possible, without direct sunlight.

Temperature: Average warmth.

Propagation: Divide off springs.

Water: Water thoroughly and provide a pebble tray.

Repotting: Repot young plants in spring. Repotting too often can inhibit the flowering of blooms.

Comments: There are two varieties of Peace Lily; the S. wallisii, which is the dwarf type, (Petite) and the S. Mauna Loa, the larger type. They both produce white flowers in spring which turn pale green as they age. The glossy leaves grow directly out of the soil. They like bottom aeration and should be raised on a plant stand or set on pot feet for best results.

STRELITZIA REGINAE Bird of Paradise, Crane Flower

S. reginae sp.

Air Humidity: Mist leaves occasionally.

Light: As much light as possible.

Temperature: Average warmth.

Propagation: Divide the clump of rhizomes at repotting time.

Water: Water thoroughly.

Repotting: Repot young plants in spring. Repotting too often can inhibit the flowering for up to 2 years. Instead, you should simply top-dress the plant with fresh potting soil.

GARDENING PASSION

Comments: The Bird of Paradise is classified in the banana family, the Musaceae. These spectacular flowers are not just a decorator's favourite, but also an exceptionally attractive landscape plant. This trunk less, compact, clustering plant, reminiscent of flying birds, produces long-lasting, intermittent blooms throughout the year. They grow on horizontal inflorescence emerging from a stout spathe. Some larger species take up to 4–5 years to flower and the rhizomes spread rapidly. The smaller species will bloom in 6 months. Fertilize them at least every couple of weeks with a general purpose water-soluble fertilizer. Their exotic blooms are prominent in both fresh and dried floral arrangements and are associated with liberty, magnificence and good perspective.

STROBILANTHES Persian Shield

Persian Shield

Air Humidity: Mist leaves frequently.

Light: Brightly lit spot but away from the direct sun.

Temperature: Average, moist warmth.

Propagation: Stem cutting.

Water: Roots should be kept moist.

Repotting: Repot in spring or summer.

Comments: The Persian Shield is a tropical shrub with foliage that are metallic purple and green in colour. The shades of shimmering metallic purple are situated within the length of the leaves and are bordered by distinct shades of green. Its underside is also coloured in purple, but of a different shade. Persian shield is a beautiful plant especially when it is young. Older plants tend to look straggly since the colour fades and the foliage becomes silvery with dark veins. his evergreen soft wood plant is comfortable in semi-shaded areas and thrives outdoors in humid surroundings and in rich, well-drained soil. It tends to get tall, so pinch it back to induce bushier foliage. Prune to shape. Position this plant so that it gets a little sun in the mornings.

SUCCULENTS

Euphorbia candelabrum (Cow Boy Cactus)

Sedum Pachyphyllum

Succulent sp.

Air Humidity: No misting necessary.

Temperature: Average warmth is ideal, but no harm will occur at slightly higher temperature.

Propagation: Take stem cuttings, offsets or leaf cuttings. Let the cuttings dry for a few days (large cuttings for 1-2 weeks) before planting.

Water: Water thoroughly when the compost begins to dry.

Repotting: Only repot in spring or summer when it becomes essential, then transfer to a slightly larger but shallow container.

Comments: Succulents are easy to grow; hence the cultivation of succulents is rewarding to both the novice grower and the hard-core enthusiast. If you are looking for an interesting mix of plants that like it both hot and dry, then the succulent is the ideal choice. Use succulents to add interest to difficult planting areas.

Succulents do not like the rich, improved soil, they like the soil on the lean side. Prepare a potting mix of lean soil, with an equal amount of coarse builder's sand. By doing this, you will create a potting media that is not too rich and drains well. Fill a container three-quarters full with the prepared mix and top off with more soil. Overwatering and ensuing plant rot is the single most common cause of plant failure. Succulents can also be planted in Rock gardens or in tiny niches. Simply stuff some soil mix into the planting pocket and add a succulent.

SYNGONIUM Goose Foot Plant

S.podophyllum
(Bronze)

Air Humidity: Mist leaves regularly.

Light: Well-lit but sunless spot.

Temperature: Average warmth.

Propagation: Take stem cuttings in spring

Water: Keep compost moist.

Repotting: Repot in spring or summer.

Comments: Syngonium podophyllum is also known as African evergreen, American evergreen, arrow head plant, arrow head vine, five fingers, goose foot, goose foot plant and goose's foot. It is a native to Mexico, Central America. It has been widely cultivated as a garden ornamental and indoor plant, creeping or climbing plant. The plants are mostly plain green and are closely related to the Philodendron. The alternately arranged leaves vary in size, shape and colour depending on their position on the plant. The lower leaves are generally arrowhead-shaped and either entirely green or with some silvery-white markings. The upper leaves are light or dark green and divided into three segments or 5-9 separate leaflets. The blooms consist of an elongated whitish spike.

S.podophyllum

The fleshy fruit are red to reddish-orange in colour. There are now new varieties with subtle shades of bronze and pink which seem to flush onto the leaf-blade from the region of the stem. The younger stems are sometimes slightly bluish-green in colour and produces a milky sap. The older plants develop a climbing habit and need the support of a moss stick. Once established, a plant will spread outwards, forming a colony and taking root wherever its stem touches the ground.

TAGETES Marigold

Tagetes

Air Humidity: Mist leaves frequently.

Light: Semi shade or bright light.

Temperature: Warm.

Propagation: Seeds.

Water: Water thoroughly and regularly.

Repotting: Not necessary.

Comments: Marigold is an annual and the most rewarding bedding plant. The original marigold is known for its pungent odour, but compensates by its constant production of robust blooms. Plant marigold among your vegetables and other plants that snails and slugs love and discover how the marigold wards off all these pests. Sow seeds in rich soil, in any month except July to September as during these months the plants expend all energies to growth instead of to the blooms. Marigolds are available in four different types. These are: African; these marigold flowers tend to be tall. French; these tend to be dwarf varieties. Triploid; these are a hybrid between African and French and are multi-coloured. Single; have long stems and look like daisies.

Marigolds are a very versatile flower. They enjoy full sun and hot days and grow well in dry or moist soil. They are often used as bedding plants and container plants. When planted in the ground, water them if the weather is dry. If they are in containers, water them daily as containers will dry out quickly. Water soluble fertilizer can be given to them once a month. Increase the number of blooms by deadheading spent blossoms. Dried seeds can be used to grow your next crop.

TERMINALIA CATAPPA

Sea Almond

The Sea Almond is also known as the Tropical Almond, West Indian Almond or Umbrella tree. On account of its almond-like fruit and propensity for growing on beaches, it is known in the English speaking Caribbean as 'Sea Almond.' It was probably brought to Jamaica by the Portuguese. It grows to 115 ft. tall with an upright, symmetrical crown and horizontal branches. The corky, light fruit has a high tolerance to salty spray. The nut

Sea Almond tree

within the within the ripe fruit is edible and is said to taste like almond. The fruity flesh which is a thick skin is also edible. As this amazing tree gets older the crown becomes more flattened to form a spreading vase shape. Its branches are distinctively arranged in tiers. The Sea Almond, used as an ornamental tree, is like a natural parasol that provides extra cool shade. It is one of our few deciduous trees that shed leaves twice a year.

The leaves turn yellow-orange and finally a deep red before shedding, giving the landscape an autumnal ambience. The whitish flowers are grown in clusters on slender spikes, very similar to the Sea Grapes. The flowers lack petals and only have a star-shaped calyx from which the fruits develop. The leaves, bark and fruits are regarded as "the medicine kit of the jungle." The tree is said to have anti-oxidative, anti-parasitic, anti-bacterial and anti- fungal properties. The dried, raw nuts are known to have an aphrodisiac effect. The fruits are almond-shaped, green, turning yellow-brown to purple when ripe. Tannin can be extracted from the fruit, bark and leaves, hence my stained garments, when as a child, I actively participated in the cracking of the fibrous shells to remove the edible kernel.

ZAMIOCULCAS ZAMIFOLIA   ZZ Plant, Fat Boy, Aroid Palm, Eternity plant

Air Humidity: No misting necessary.

Light: Grows in bright, indirect light or low light, but produces more leaves in brighter light.

Temperature: Average warmth.

Propagation: Propagate with leaf cuttings or root tubers. Propagating by leaf may take many months before it produces new growth.

Water: Water once every week.

Soil: Plant in soil that retains water, but also drains well. The rhizomes will rot if the soil is soggy. Use a cactus soil mix and add perlite or pebbles to the potting mix.

Zamioculcas Zamifolia
Zee Zee Plant

Repotting: Repot if needed in spring.

Comments: The ZZ plant (*Zee-Zee*) is a succulent and is quite an exciting, versatile and stunning house plant. It is one of the newest house plants to enter our homes. Known for its high resistance to insects and diseases, the ZZ plant is capable of cleaning the indoor air and making it healthier for us. This slow and low-growing plant is a native to eastern Africa. The thick, long and upright stems contain hundreds of round, glossy dark-green leaves. During the summer, small flowers may bloom at the base of the plant. The large tubers act as a reservoir for feeding the plant with water as needed. It is easy care for and low maintenance has made it a favourite. Too much direct sunlight will burn the foliage. Fertilize the ZZ plant with half-diluted, balanced liquid fertilizer once every season.

CHAPTER TWO

CARING FOR HOUSE PLANTS

"Just living is not enough, One must have sunshine, freedom and a little flower." **Anonymous**

There are a few fundamental principles that gardeners depend on for the production of beautiful gardens. These include;

Knowing the soil type Study the soil type, test the soil on your property and aim at improving the quality and the drainage if necessary.

Studying the sunny and shaded areas Note the areas that enjoy different levels of sunlight as the sun pattern changes throughout the day, the season and the year.

Studying the seasons Plants grow best in a particular season, so consult a botanist, research via the internet or books, or observe the best times for planting. Operate simultaneously with the seasons and plant and reap accordingly.

Selecting suitable plants for the available space Place plants with similar characteristics and needs together allowing enough space to prevent overcrowding as they grow.

Observing your gardens Look for potential problems such as developing pests infestation and plants which show particular needs.

Doing some experiments Be innovative and move away from the norm. Do the extreme and await the amazing results.

Schefflera (Umbrella Plant)

GARDENING PASSION

There is something intriguing and satisfying about growing a plant in a container and keeping it indoors to serve as an unbeatable decorating accessory. There are instances when these plants are given names as they hold prominent positions in the household. Most are instrumental in absorbing potentially harmful gases and cleaning the air inside buildings. The foliage of indoor plants are capable of removing low levels of pollution while the roots remove air pollutants at higher concentrations. It should be noted that no plant has been found to remove tobacco smoke nor is any one plant good at removing all indoor air pollutants. Plants are fed from rainfall and from nutrients supplied from the soil. The main problem house plants encounter is the lack of water. Many house plants and those in the offices, often suffer this fate. Mistakes such as overwatering can lead to disease and root rot, while under watering can cause other severe effects. Other factors such as soil composition, humidity, seasonal changes and temperature changes can also prove to be detrimental. Plants with green, large and shiny leaves are much more tolerant and may survive in indifferent conditions. The variegated types need more care, while those with thick leaves require less watering. House plants are classified in four groups: *Foliage House Plants, Flowering House Plants, Flowering Pot Plant and Cacti.*

Foliage House Plants

Aspidistra

Foliage plants are grown for their foliage as the attraction lies in the beauty of each leaf. Since foliage plants are not comprised of only all-green plants, a year round multi-coloured display can be achieved with plants such as Crotons, Caladiums and Dieffenbachia,. The Rubber Plant and the Ficus Benjamina are other well-used house and office plants. While some foliage plants can be delicate, others are known to have cast-iron constitution. Many of these house plants are capable of out living their owners.

Flowering House Plants

Begonia

Prior to the introduction of the potted plants in the house, flowers were cut and placed in a vase to enhance the beauty of the interior. Today the whole aspect of a flowering plant in a pot has added a new variation and is much more fascinating. A group of house plants that will bloom all year round includes the popular Orchid, Anthurium and the Peace Lily. These blooms last for several weeks. Annuals will also fill your space with welcome splashes of colour all year round. A wise selection of plants will see your home illuminated with blooms all year round. When some plants are not blooming they may not necessarily be attractive. Notwithstanding, some varieties have leaves and formations that are so beautiful that they are worth being on display.

Flowering Pot Plants

Poinsettia

The flowering potted plants are temporary or seasonal residents in the home. They are referred to as 'gift plants' or 'florists' plants. Most of these are thrown away once they have faded while others can be kept for another season. The lack of permanence is a disadvantage but that does not deter the home owner from purchasing or cultivating these plants. The irresistible Poinsettia made ready for the bountiful Christmas season is one such plant. It is joined by the Gloxinia, Chrysanthemum and the Hyacinth. With proper management the Poinsettia can remain showy for a few months and can provide repeated display. Flowering house plants need bright, cool conditions and moist compost. They need more light than the foliage ones do. Mist the leaves regularly and avoid warm air and draughts as these are their biggest enemies.

Cacti

Rubella senilis

Cacti are plants that thrive in areas of high temperatures and low water availability. They however, relish some attention and care. There are Cacti in millions of homes and the expectation is that they will show signs of growth and development and that they will eventually bloom. Cacti can withstand several hours of sunshine without suffering adverse effects. They seem so comfortable on the windowsill and thrive best in small pots.

PLANTS IN THE OFFICE

Dieffenbachia; a popular office plant

There are numerous displays of lush foliage and flowering plants that have transformed thousands of offices and boardrooms into pleasant surroundings. Here, the plants are generally subjected to five days of regulated temperature and light. This regime is followed by two days of reduced or higher temperature and even complete darkness. The foliage plants cope better than the flowering plants in this environment. The enclosed air-conditioned offices are loaded with chemicals that are spewed from new carpets, fresh paints, upholstery, computers and plastics. It has been suggested that everyone should have a plant in the office where one spends most of the day. It is also recommended that one potted plant be placed in a 100 sq. ft. of floor space to help improve the air quality.

Research has shown that;

- The more plants the staff can see the fewer sick leave applications are handed in.

- Greenery reduces office workers' fatigues, dry throat, headache, cough and dry skin.

- Workers know that plants are healthy and are likely to evaluate their own health optimistically.

- Plants reduce workers' stress and improve their reaction times.

- Workers in a green office generally have more normal blood pressure and less mental fatigue.

- Those who work alongside plants perform better than those in plant free offices.

- Plants help reduce distractions as they help to reduce office noise.

- Plants contribute to interior humidity by adding moisture to the air through transpiration and evaporation.

- Water indoor and office plants regularly with enough water that will flush the plant and the roots. If you overwater them they could die. The plants have had enough when the water drains into the drip saucer under the pot. Use pots with drainage holes. Procure saucers made for potted plants. These saucers will catch the excess water and prevent the wetting of the floor. On the saucer, raise the pot on three pot feet or on small stones. Set the potted plant in a decorated container without draining holes, if so, then raise the pot so that it will not sit in the water. Misting delivers a steady and constant stream of water, more so to the foliage. Maybe Tuesdays and Fridays are ideal days to water.

The blooming
Gold Dust Dracaena

GARDENING PASSION

TEMPERATURE, HUMIDITY and LIGHT

Temperature Some plants do require cooler conditions than we ordinarily find in our homes. While house plants tolerate normal temperature fluctuations, excessively low or high temperatures may cause plant failure, retarded growth, spindly appearance, less resistance to disease, foliage damage and insect attack. A sudden temperature drop can injure plants and temperatures below 50° F for extended periods may cause permanent damage. Symptoms of temperature damage starts with wilting, yellowing of leaves and leaf drop. Foliage house plants grow best between 70° and 80° F during the day and from 60°-68° F at night. Most flowering house plants prefer the same daytime range, but grow best at night-time in temperature ranging from 55°-60° F. Lower night time temperatures induce physiological recovery from moisture loss, intensify flower colour, build new tissues and prolong flower life in some plants. A cooler temperature at night is actually more desirable for some plant growth rather than higher temperature. Flowering plants will retain blossoms longer if lower temperature is provided. A good rule of thumb is to keep the night-time temperatures between 10°-15° F lower than the day temperature. Keep plants away from temperature extremes or fluctuations produced by air conditioning vents, fan, clothes dryers and the top of the television, refrigerator and heater. Fresh air lowers the temperature in hot weather.

Humidity Next to light and proper soil, there is nothing more important to the well being of plants than moisture. There are a number of ways of combating the lack of moisture and this is by increasing the humidity in the air. Place plants in a pebble tray and refill with water as necessary. Group plants. Plants requiring high humidity are best placed in the bathroom or kitchen where it aught to be a little more humid than the rest of the house. Water plants regularly. Mulch plants periodically. Mist plants in the

Pebble tray

mornings so that their foliage will be dry before nightfall. Misting also washes off the dust that might have accumulated on the leaves. Use a mister for the job and not the garden hose. Do not mist when the sun is on the plants.

Light

Plants vary considerably in their light requirements. Some plants need direct sunlight, while others will grow under lower light intensity. Plants use light to make food during photosynthesis; when the green leaves make complex sugar. Matching a plant to the light it requires is very important. The lighting guide talks about full sun, bright but sunless, semi-shade, shade and deep shade. Light classification is often found on packaged plant labels.

Semi-shade plants require some sun and some shade too, so give them a little of both worlds. The lower the light, the slower the plant grows. The morning sun is mild, but the evening sun can be very hot and can scorch some plants. Some plants are adaptable to whatever light conditions they are offered. Plants are phototropic, hence they grow towards the light source, so turn your potted plants every time you water them as this will maintain an even foliage growth. A plant should not be moved suddenly from a shady spot to a sunny spot, but should be acclimatized gradually. Plants with variegated leaves require more light than purely green leaves. Flowering plants need more light than foliage plants and the more light they get the more blooms they will produce. Therefore, ensure that the required daily period of light is provided. Rooms and offices that are always lit are not the most ideal settings for indoor plants since most plants grow at nights and the dark conditions would be absent. Also white walls of offices and homes reflect more light than coloured walls.

The Dracaena requires ample light for the production of lush blooms

WATER REQUIREMENTS

Water to mimic the raindrops

Too Much Water   Did you know that too much water can drown your plant? Roots take in air from spaces in the soil. If the spaces are filled with water and the plant does not get the air it requires it will drown. Pants that are drenched will stop forming new leaves. Their youngest leaves will turn dark green, the edge of the other leaves turn yellow and their lower leaves wilt and fall. The affected stems will then become mushy, rot and die. Soil should therefore be wet thoroughly but the water should not be allowed to sit there. A well-drained soil mixture is essential for ease of watering as heavy soil mix holds too much water and causes the plant to rot at the crown. Do not allow your potted plants to sit in saucers containing water, raise the pot or pour off the excess water. Ensure that the drainage holes are open. Touch and feel for the moisture level, by putting your finger down to 1in. into the pot soil. If the soil surface feels dry, then it is time to water.

Too Little Water   The plants that are deprived of water will exhibit signs of decline, but you may be able to save them if your response is timely. You would have observed that the plant growth has slowed, its foliage has wilted, the tips of the leaves have become brown and the lower leaves turned yellow, go dry and die. The dry soil would also shrink away from the container, causing grave damage to the root system. If you add water and it runs out of the drain holes immediately, it is an indication that the soil was completely dried out. A dried or wilted plant can be treated by using the 'leach' method; immersing the plant in a bucket of water for about 30 minutes. You may also water thoroughly then serve small portions of water in three servings, thrice per day until recovery. If you will be away from home, you need to ensure that the plants do not suffer dehydration. The wick or self-watering system is an option to try. To ensure that the pot is not sitting directly in the water elevate it on pot feet before placing it in the saucer.

Watering Guide

Water preferences: Most plants prefer to live in soil that is moist but not wet. Annuals and vegetables like it moist, succulents like it a bit dry, while most herbs like it to dry out a little in between watering.

- **Moisture levels:** Before watering check to see if the plant really needs it. Poorly prepared potting mix becomes hard and will not absorb water efficiently if left to completely dry out.

- **Sufficient water:** Ensure that the pots are never filled with soil higher than an inch from the top. This will allow you to fill it to the brim and let the water soak down to the roots.

- **Time of day:** Plant roots are more receptive to watering in the morning. Water in the late evening only if you are forced to do so. Do not water during the heat of the day.

- **Leaf preference:** The leaves of most plants are to be misted when the plant is being watered. Plants with hairy leaves detest water on their leaves. Wet leaves can lead to an increased chance of fungus, mildew and other diseases.

- **After the rainfall:** Foliage, especially those big leaves can act like umbrellas and will keep the water from getting to the soil below. Some plants need to be watered after a shower of rain.

- **Once may not be enough:** Heat, wind and dry air can quickly parch plants. Terra cotta pots, hanging baskets, plastic, concrete and metal pots all can dry out fast. on a hot, windy, summer day. Plants growing in these containers may need to be watered twice in one day.

- **Water temperatures:** Water from the hose and watering can are likely to have a change in temperature. Use water at room temperature. Cold water and ice cubes can blight plants and should not be used. Tap water should stand for 12-24 hours to allow the chlorine to escape.

- **The right tools:** Be kind. Select the right tool such as watering cans and nozzles. If a hose is used, engage the right nozzle for the job.

GROOM YOUR PLANTS

Plants breathe through their leaves and should not be allowed to be stifled with unsightly dirt and injurious dust. Indoor plants love to be placed outdoors during a light shower of rain. Give your Rubber Plant, Philodendron and Sanseviera a sponge bath with tepid water and a small amount of liquid detergent. Sponge or spray the solution gently on the leaves and then rinse with clean water to ensure that no soapy residue is left. Polish or spray them lightly, not with cooking oil, but with one of the commercially available leaf shine. This polish is not harmful and contains an insecticide that protects the plants from invading insects. Groom those plants with hairy leaves such as the African violet and the Kalanchoe (Velvet Plant) by brushing with a fine, soft brush. Be gentle, rough handling will damage the leaves.

Grooming Tips

Plants naturally grow towards the light causing them to look lopsided or even to topple over. Prevent this by giving the plant a quarter turn each time you water.

• Shape plants by pruning or by pinching with your thumb and forefinger. This will force the plant to branch out and become bushier. Start training while the plant is still young.

• Remove faded flowers, leaves or bracts and any damaged part of the plant, so that the plant can put energy into growth instead of healing the injured parts. Remove and pot offsets and pups.

Dirty, dull and dusty before grooming

Sparkling clean after grooming

Stake the Plants

Stake and support plants to keep upright plants in an upright position. Stake to keep fruits and vegetables off the ground to reduce fruit rot and loss. Staked plants are easier to spray or dust for insects and disease. They are easier to harvest than those sprawling on the ground. The method of support should be decided before setting the plants in the garden. Wooden or metal stakes 5-6 ft. high may be required for taller plants while shrubs and vegetables will require shorter and branch-like stakes. Wooden stakes should be at least 2 in. in diameter. Avoid the use of lumber that has been treated with chemicals.

Climbing Philodendron

Drive the stakes about 12 in. into the ground beside the plants that need support. When the plant is about 18 in. high it should be tied to the stake by using a piece of fabric, noting that the use of fabric will prevent damage to the stem. When the plant reaches to the top of the stake, it is wise to pinch off the growing tip where applicable. This will force side branches.

Metal stakes can be of a smaller diameter and will last many years. The metal should be wrapped with burlap or coir. Tie branches to the stake with soft cord, sisal or fabric, by first tying twine to the stake and then looping it close, but loosely around the plant. Straight limbs used as stakes can be cut from nearly any local tree. The fence stake plant is often used for this purpose, it may however, make roots and grow right there. The bamboo makes a good stake. Decorative stakes are available on the market and will add to the décor. You can make and decorate your own stakes.

Tie plants at intervals to support growth

GARDENING PASSION

LET THE FRESH AIR IN

Open the windows and let the clean, fresh air in

Proper ventilation is the key to indoor growing success and should be of optimal concern. Without an abundant supply of fresh air, close to that which the plants would have received outdoor, your efforts at cultivating plants indoors will prove futile. The amount of ventilation that is required depends largely on the size of the space in which they are housed. The more plants you have in the room, the more important good ventilation becomes.

- Fresh air strengthens the stems and leaves. Fresh air gives blooms a brighter appearance.

- Fresh air removes traces of toxic vapours that can be damaging to growing plants.

If proper ventilation is lacking then the pores of the leaves will become clogged and the plant will eventually die. Maintain a free movement of air so that the poisonous gases can escape. My response as to the beauty of my indoor plants is that I throw open those doors and windows and let the fresh air flow through. Louvred windows or a fan to circulate the air will be helpful too. Indoor plants are sensitive to unnatural or blended gas, so steer the plants away from this danger. Plants that are exposed to poisonous gases will refuse to flower and will drop flower buds and foliage. Ensure that the areas where the plants are placed enjoy proper ventilation and have sufficient air circulation. Although it may be possible to grow plants in poorly ventilated rooms, they would be larger and healthier if they had a fresh supply of air. The roots of plants also need to be ventilated. This can be done by using a hand fork to turn over the surface of the soil to the depth of an inch, allowing air to get in among the roots.

(1) Osmocote   (2) Bloom Booster   (3) Urea   (4) 20.20.20   (5) Orchid Bloom Booster

FEED THOSE PLANTS

It is with good intention that plants are potted in the best potting mix. The pots are filled with the richest soil collected from the compost heap. It is inevitable however, that this same soil will eventually need to be supplemented. Plants that are planted in the ground are naturally fed, as the soil in the open is constantly being replenished with decaying vegetable matter and natural fertilizers from the rain. These plants are capable of sending their roots far and wide in search of nutrients while their counterparts in pots are totally dependent on us for food. Nutrients escape each time the plant is watered, so fertilizer should be fed to the plants to replenish those depleted nutrients. Plants require 16 nutritive elements to survive. A lack of any nutrient will result in deficiencies such as yellowing of the leaves and stems, stunted growth and pre-mature death of the flower or fruit.

Three of the primary elements are Nitrogen, Phosphorous and Potassium. These ingredients are found in varying degrees in all organic and animal manure. Nitrogen (N) is responsible for the green colour and growth of foliage and stems. Phosphorous (P) is responsible for the production of buds, flowers and strong roots. Potassium (K) is necessary for the overall health and sturdiness of the plant. Soil testing reveals that most soils are deficient in several key nutrients; hence the formulation of commercial fertilizers, some of which are formulated for specific plants and purposes. These are available in liquid, sticks and granular. Most fertilizers are soluble in water and are fed to the plants in a liquid form at intervals in the recommended portion. They are odourless, lightweight and are scientifically prepared.

GARDENING PASSION

When to Fertilize

Most flowering plants do not require fertilizer while they are in flower. Annuals grow very quickly and need fertilizer every three weeks before blooms appear. However, others whose growth continue while they bloom will need fertilizer. Allow your plants to establish themselves before you apply fertilizer. A newly potted plant should be given time to spread its roots and to grow new roots to absorb the fertilizer. Some plants experience a period of rest or dormancy. Wait until the first new leaves are well established before applying fertilizer. Succulents and Cacti should be fed at four-month intervals. As a general rule, apply fertilizer to most long-term plants every 1-2 months while growth is rapid. Use an all purpose fertilizer and add additional nutrients for specific plant types.

Plants that grow rapidly utilize the nutrients in the limited growing media very quickly. When this is consumed the plant begins to show signs of food deprivation; becoming pale and yellow. Leaves that yellow at the edges and between the veins show signs of iron deficiency. In this case the plant requires a complete dose of all the required nutrients. An excessive amount of fertilizer can be detrimental to the general well being of the plant. It will cause the plants to develop robust, deep green leaves, which may seem favourable, but will later result in yellow, brown and pre-mature leaf fall. When detected, stop feeding with fertilizer and prune the plant. Leach the plant a few times.

Feeding Tips

Plants that require more light will require more frequent feeding.

- Do not feed a dormant plant; wait until the plant is actively growing before you feed.

- Do not exceed the recommended dose; it is even wiser to reduce the amount.

- Fertilize after you water as fertilizer is best applied to wet soil.

- When potting soil is fresh, the plants will not need any fertilizer. But after about two months the plant would have consumed the nutrients in the soil. Fertilize for continued healthy growth.

INCREASE YOUR STOCK

Propagating Dendrobium Orchids

Your stock of plants can be increased by propagation. Plants can be propagated by asexual or sexual means. Sexual propagation involves starting plants from seeds, while asexual propagation refers to multiplication of vegetative plant parts such as shoots, roots and leaves, or from specialized organs such as bulbs, tubers and corms. Budding, grafting and air layering are also methods of vegetative propagation which

seem superior to seeds as the resultant plants are identical to the parent and mature much quicker than plants grown from seeds.

1. Propagate to make multiple plants from a single plant. 2. Create a young, attractive plant from an old, leggy one. 3. Capture the unique, attractive features of a plant.

Factures to ensure success: Select and use only healthy, vigorous source plants.   Use the most appropriate techniques. Propagate during the right season. Protect propagation material from heat, drying and wilting. Use fresh seeds and other materials soon after they are prepared. Give newly propagated plants extra care during the early development.

Seeds Seeds are the most common and most convenient method of plant propagation. Seeding is time consuming when planting is done on a large scale. They are the means whereby hybrids are obtained, since it is impossible to cross breed tubers, slips or grafts to produce new varieties of plants. When raising seeds, select the strongest plants and reduce the number of flowers. In this way the parent plant will concentrate its energy in the production of quality seeds for the best flowers. Seeds germinate best when planted as soon as the fruits are ripe.

Palm seedlings

Store dry seeds, not ready for planting in an airtight container. When ready to propagate place large seeds in a moist medium, e.g. sand and coconut fiber or sand and peat moss. Some seeds will germinate in a few days, others take a longer time because the coat is tough and does not allow moisture to penetrate readily. Hasten germination by soaking seeds overnight in tepid water before planting.

Sow the Seeds

Prepare the soil and sow the seeds in garden beds or in containers. Cover large seeds with a thin layer of soil but leave small seeds uncovered. Many annuals and perennials can be sown directly in the ground, but some should be started in containers then transplanted. Use plant markers to help identify the variety and location of the seeds. Water the seedbeds gently by using a water can or a fine-mist nozzle to avoid washing away the seeds. Cover the seedbed with a light layer of mulch to help retain moisture. Unless it rains, water the seedbeds every day until the seedlings are well established. When plants are large enough to handle, remove these seedlings to a suitable location.

Spores Seeding

Spores

Spores are seeds produced on the underside of ferns. Examine the leaves, if the dots are plump and seem ready to burst, it is time to plant the spores. Place the portion of leaf with unopened spores on the surface of damp soil in a pot. Cover the rim of the pot with a sheet of clear glass, place the pot on a pebble tray. No surface watering is necessary. Within 4-14 days you should notice a translucent green film on the surface of the medium, a sign that germination has taken place. Remove glass cover gradually; over a number of days. When spore lings are about 1 in. it is time to pot them individually.

Rhizomes or Runners

Rhizomes are shoots thrown off by the parent plant below the soil surface. Expect this from the Cannas, Sansevieria, Bird of Paradise and Ginger Lily family. Scratch the surface of the soil and the rhizomes are sitting there awaiting their time to surface. Cut off the new plants and pot them.

Eye Plants

Would you like a plant of the rare Dieffenbachia ? Then you need to select a plump eye and cut this off in a slanting direction. Plant the cutting in a shallow pot and cover with an inch of sandy soil. No need to water, just keep this plant shaded. In a few weeks you will be greeted by the appearance of new leaves.

Root Cuttings

Some plants are stubborn and even selfish. Well, let's get even with these hardy fellows and take them from the roots. Remove a few inches of the soil and cut off a portion of the root. Cut away most of the roots and plant the stump in rich soil. Keep moist and shaded. After three months look out for the new growth. The Allamanda and the June Rose are two such plants.

Cane Cuttings

This method is often used with the Crystal Anthurium, Dracaena and Dieffenbachia. The trunk is cut in several 2-3 in. long segments. Look for a leaf bud that must be planted in an upward position. Await the new growth.

Offsets   Bromeliads, Cacti and some succulents are known to produce side shoots. Cut off shoots as near as possible to the parent plant. Pot or plant each new plant. Keep shaded until established.

Stem Cuttings   Do stem cuttings in spring and summer. Choose sturdy, healthy, non-flowering shoots and plant these as soon as they are cut. Note however, that Succulent cuttings should be drained for several days before planting.

Pups   Some plants form several clumps, (daughters or pups) as they mature. When the 'pup' is big enough, remove it carefully using a sharp knife. Water sparingly and watch for new growth.

Bulbs   A large bulb can be divided to obtain more than one plants. With a clean knife cut through the base vertically to the tip of the bulb. Start each portion in a shallow pot or seed box. Try this with your Lilies and Gladiolas. Bulbs multiply underground. After each blooming season dig for these extra treasures.

Rooting In Water   Crotons root readily in water. These will surprise you with roots if you stick a stem on a kenzan or stand it in a vase with water. Remove the leaves that are likely to rest in the water as these will rot. Once the roots are established you can remove the plant to the pot or garden bed.

Plantlets   The Spider plant produces lots of plantlets. If the plantlets are without roots just set these in a pot of compost and they will produce roots. As soon as roots are established they are ready to be planted.

Leaf Cuttings   This technique can be applied to the whole leaf or part of a leaf. It is often applied to the Peperomia, some Succulents, African Violet and Sansevieria among others. No rooting hormone is needed for these soft stems.

Ground Layering   Bend a low growing branch to the ground and new roots will form where it is touching the soil. Pare off an inch of the bark on the underside to help the plant root more quickly. Dust on some rooting hormone and cover with about 3 in. of soil. Pin it down to keep the branch in place. Keep it watered until new roots are formed. When there is a good root system in place, cut from the connected branch and plant.

Grafting or Budding   **Grafting** is the fusing of the tissues of two different plants. It is carried out with plants of the same family and is limited to hard wood plants. It is often used in horticulture. **Budding** is a form of grafting. A shoot is selected and is grafted onto the stock of another type. The tissues of both plants must be kept alive till the graft has taken. March and April are the more successful months for grafting as the sap is most active at this time. Graft on an overcast day and work quickly as both bark and bud will lose their sap when exposed to air.

GARDENING PASSION

The Benefits of Grafting

Ease of propagation: To reproduce species of some plants that are difficult to propagate.

Hybrid breeding: To speed the growth of hybrid trees and flowers.

Dwarfing: To produce smaller trees which are known to bear fruits in a short time.

Changing cultivars: To change the species to a more a desirable type. Citrus is often used.

Assorted fruits: To produce plants with two or more fruits growing on one tree.

Grafting Techniques

Cleft: A tongue is made of the scion which is inserted into a slit on the top of the stock. The tongue is positioned so that the tissues are resting against each other.

Side: This is done by applying a slantingly cut shoot of the scion to a similarly shaped slice made along the top of the stock.

Veneer: This is quite similar to side grafting except that both stock and scion are in wedge shapes which fit perfectly together.

Patch: Remove rectangular piece of bark from the stock. Make an identical size and shape scion with one bud in centre. Fit the patch over the portion laid bare of stock.

Bind the stock and scion with waxed tape to prevent the entry of water, moisture or air.

Circumposing or Air Layering

This technique is used on plants that are difficult root or have become tall and 'leggy.' Circumposing is used to propagate woody plants with stiff, upright limbs that can be difficult to propagate by ground layering. This is used to stimulate root growth at some point on a stem while the branch is still attached to the mother plant. This is best done in spring when the sap is active and the plants are growing vigorously.

Cut and peel away the bark

Hold coir in place

Twist and tie

Rooted plant

How to Circumpose Plants

Select a portion of the stem where the roots will develop and carefully remove the extra leaves.

- Use a clean, sharp knife to make a 1-1½ in. upward cut, starting below a leaf node.

- Remove the entire circumference of bark by cutting a ring. The woody portion can be left exposed to air for 7-10 days.

- Use a paintbrush and apply rooting powder to the callus formed.

- Place some saturated coir or moss on a strip of clear plastic.

- Hold the moss in position, twist and fasten this securely at the top and bottom to form an airtight sleeve. Secure with tape or twine.

- Cover this with a strip of aluminium foil to keep the moisture in.

- Within weeks a mass of white worm-like roots will be visible through the clear plastic.

- Sever from the parent plant by cutting below the plastic sleeve. You may use a hand-saw to do this. Remove the plastic and expose the new root .

- Tease out the roots without breaking them. Plant the new plant and offer extra care during this period.

- Keep the new plant out of direct sunlight for two to three weeks to minimize shock.

Cover with aluminium foil

GARDENING PASSION

PESTS AND DISEASES

Now that your vegetables and flowers are thriving, it is prime time for the hoards of insects, pests and diseases to invade your little piece of paradise. The Peace lily, Hostas and Cannas are caviar to slugs and snails so be on the look out for them. The culprits may be those destructive insects or dreaded plant diseases. Whatever the experiences, there is always a solution.

Hibiscus plant infested by the Pink Mealy Bug

Before they do, let us be pro-active and prevent this scary attack. Remove all debris, rotting wood and empty containers as these make fine hide-outs for snails, ants, slugs and mildew. Cover the compost heaps and drums. Rid the garden of insects and flies as they are often responsible for infesting those healthy plants. The dreaded Pink Mealy Bug is capable of wiping out your entire crop. They suck the juice from the host plant and inject a toxic saliva that causes malformation of leaves and fruits and terminates growth. Pesticides are ineffective but cutting and burning the host material is the best solution.

Have fun with that lizard Zack, but avoid touching those plants

Keep the slugs and snails away
Slugs are best described as snails without shells. They are related to the oysters and clam family. They love the garden, lay their eggs in the debris and will create havoc in the garden. They seem very loving but to the horticulturist they are the most unkind culprits. Crush several garlic cloves, add water and steep overnight. Strain and spray on plants every few days or after rainfall. This bad tasting spray will deter slugs and snails. Remove the slugs at night or early in the morning when they are out on the rampage for food. Handpick and throw them in the fire or set slug bait in their path.

- Create a barrier made of copper around the garden to prevent the slugs from entering.

- Scatter coffee grounds, crushed eggshells or coarse sand around the garden bed. They hate to crawl over the rough surface, it will cut their skin and cause them to dehydrate.

- Drown them in soapy water, crush them or spray them with household ammonia diluted to a 5-10 % solution.

- Trap them in layers of newspaper soaked in beer.

- Sprinkle household salt on them; this will dissolve them.

Slugs in the garden

One destructive snail

Home-made Treatment

Milk and Water Control mildew and fungi by combining 1 cup cow's milk with 9 cups water. Spray the affected plants twice weekly. It is believed the milk has a direct germicidal effect as well as indirectly stimulating the plants to become more resistant.

Water Only A constant spray of water can knock off and drown aphids and caterpillars. Spray the under-side of the leaves where most insects and pests converge.

Dishwashing Liquid, Bleach and Water Mix together 1 tablespoon household bleach, 1 tablespoon dishwashing liquid and 1 gallon water. Spray insects and pests including ants. It is best to spray plants on a cloudy day or in the early morning when they are not in direct sunlight.

Baking Soda, Oil and Water Mix 3 tablespoons baking soda, 2½ tablespoons horticultural oil, 1 gallon water and shake well. Spray the infected plants and kill the powdery mildew. This is a fungal disease that affects some vegetables, squash and strawberries. It affects many fruit trees too.

CHAPTER THREE

GARDENING IN ASSORTED CONTAINERS

The pot, jug, basket or basin which holds the soil and plant is the foundation of any container garden. Container gardens have exploded in popularity and are no longer confined to the clay pot. Containers for growing plants can be made from organic or inorganic material.

The largest and healthiest Anthuruim bloom that I had ever seen was one that was growing under the partial shade of a sprawling tree. The roots were set in the decaying stump of a nearby tree that was apparently hewn down years ago; a whimsical container that was. Take a look around and you will find that there are umpteen containers from which to choose. A good container however, should have a cavity large enough to provide room for soil and roots, sufficient headspace for proper watering, bottom or side drainage holes and should be appropriate for the size plant. These may be made from clay, ceramics, plastic, fiberglass, wood, bamboo, wicker, aluminium, copper, brass, marble or concrete. Pots and containers are receptacles used to house plants. The concept of these can be a little confusing. Basket type containers aught to be lined with plastic. Wooden containers should be treated with a sealant or several coats of oil paint. An inch or two of pebbles are used to floor the base of the wooden container. If containers are placed outdoors to enjoy the full flush of the rainfall then one should feel free to bore holes in them when necessary.

A Container may be a receptacle with no holes at the base or sides. It may be used for potting or displaying one or more arrangements or for holding several pots. One main problem with these containers is that if used as a pot the excess water cannot run off. Therefore you should punch holes in them. Plastic containers are quite light, easy to handle and have become the standard containers of choice for florists because they are relatively inexpensive and quite attractive. Plastic pots are easy to sterilize, are not as porous as the clay pots and need less frequent watering. Keep your eyes open for original containers as you travel through the countryside. Oftentimes the items you find just need a little revamping. Sterilize the containers in a solution of 1 part bleach to 10 parts water to kill any mould and bacteria that may be present.

Containers

GARDENING PASSION

Pot-holder

A Pot Holder (Pot Hider) (Cachepot) is a receptacle with no drainage holes and a waterproof base. It is used for holding and hiding one or more pots. These holders are available in different sizes and shapes and are made of opaque glass, plastic, stainless steel, ceramic, wicker or fiberglass. The pot holder should be a little wider and a little higher than the pot it is concealing.

A Pot is a receptacle with a drainage hole or a number of holes at the base or sides. It is used for displaying arrangements or for potting one or more plants.

Clay or ceramic containers, unglazed or glazed, are more classy and their use seem to take precedence over other pots. Additionally, clay pots absorb and lose moisture through their walls and nutrients accumulate in the pores, resulting in the greatest accumulation of roots next to the walls of the clay pot.

Clay pots also provide excellent aeration for plant roots and are considered to be the healthiest type of containers. These may be designed with or without drainage holes. Those without drainage holes are mostly used for the aesthetics. One negative aspect of clay pots is that they are easily broken.

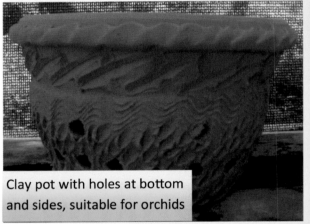

Clay pot with holes at bottom and sides, suitable for orchids

Decorated clay pot

Unglazed Ceramic   These clay pots are superb for large or small growing plants and are ideal for specimen and Bonsai plants. They are fired in the kiln to obtain a flat finish and toughness. They maintain the natural colour of the clay used and do not have a sheen.

Glazed Ceramic   These clay containers have a characteristic sheen and subtle variations in colour, achieved by throwing salt into the kiln during firing. They are impervious to moisture. Use them in the most sophisticated fashion. Place them around the garden or group them among your antiques in the house as they lend a touch of class to any occasion. Maybe your jar is a family heirloom, is sentimental and bears a multitude of treasured memories. Mine does.

Fiberglass Pots These are lightweight containers that mimic heavier stone-like containers. They are resistant to heat, cold, wet weather, corrosion and leaching.

Wicker Baskets These make excellent containers. To prolong their lifespan you may line them with plastic or paint the baskets with clear varnish or lacquer. Avoid hanging them by the handles. These woven baskets are very appealing and lend a country flavour to displays. They are light and have a rustic, invaluable informality.

Wire Baskets Wire baskets were introduced for the hanging basket gardener. Line them with plastic and fill with coir. They are stronger than wicker and are often suspended from trees or brackets. They perform well in exuberant planting schemes.

Plastic Baskets Put into service those racks and dish drainers. These are cheaper and more individualized. Use these in the water garden and to store small garden tools.

Urns are available in various materials and in different shapes and sizes. Most are constructed in two pieces, wherein the base is separated from the bowl. Those made of concrete are extremely heavy. Urns form breath-taking focal points and add formality to any garden setting.

Bamboo Troughs Bamboo is tough and can be painted or left in its natural colour. Use them jointed or cut them vertically and lay them flat. Drill holes and hang them on trees or columns. Use them for upright or for trailing plants.

Wooden Boxes Wooden boxes are attractive and blend nicely with

outdoor or indoor settings. They are quite susceptible to rot. Raise your boxes off the ground to lessen the moisture absorbed and keep them

away from the direct onslaught of the rain. Line the box with plastic or place a sturdy "same shaped" container inside the box. Stand small plastic pots in this box.

Large Plastic Pots   A large pot makes a bold statement. Some are large enough to be elevated gardens or to accommodate large specimen plants. Place a number of small flowering plants in the ample space they provide.

Small Plastic Pots   Small containers look their best in clusters. Start your seeds or nurture your seedlings or cuttings in them. Your friends will welcome a garden gift of a plant in these pots.

Hand Painted Pots   I was convinced that the blooming Crown of Thorns look their best in white pots, so I gathered and painted many pots. The transformation was most satisfying. Paint those discoloured pots, revamp them.

Saucers   Use saucers to capture the loose soil and dripping water that escape from the bottom of pots. These are sometimes sold with the pots. Clear plastic saucers may be used. These will not get damp. Handle them with care as damaged ones will result in leakage. Terra cotta saucers will get damp and should be placed only on surfaces that will not be affected.

Pot Feet These are used to raise the level of the pot in the saucer thus ensuring that the container is not sitting in water. Raised pot facilitates better drainage, provides air circulation, hastens evaporation from the bottom of the pot and prevents staining the surface on which the pot is placed. These are available in decorative designs that highlight garden related features like birds, frogs or rabbits. Use broken bricks, wooden blocks, stones or bottle covers as pot feet.

Preparing Containers

New clay pots must be soaked overnight in order to remove potentially harmful soluble chemicals. Wash all used or dirty pots thoroughly to remove any diseased organisms. Scrape away crusty deposits of salts or soil and sterilize the containers.

When to Pot those Plants

Spring is always the best season to pot or repot plants. This will give the roots plenty of time to become established before the onset of the rest period. You may want to repot a plant into a more attractive container or you may opt to repot a plant that has outgrown its current container.

Selecting the Pot Size

When transplanting plants choose a pot just a little larger than the previous one, as too large a difference may result in the plant suffering shock. You can move from a 4 in.-6 in. pot, but not a 4 in.-8 in. pot. This will retard the general growth.

Recognize and attend to root-bound plants

Root bound plants are potted plants which have outgrown their containers and their roots have started to circle around the inside or poke

A matted mass of roots, no soil

out through the drain holes of the pot they are in. Examine the plants and see if they seem stunted, deformed, pale, dull or top heavy. Look out for the plants' general decline or if water drains quickly through the pot holes. If any of these signs are present then it is high time to repot those plant. By repotting you will accomplish three tasks in one move. You will eliminate the restricted root space, replenish the depleted potting soil and you will make the plant look better in a container more in scale with its larger size.

REPOTTING

Spread the fingers of one hand over the soil surface. Invert and gently squeeze from the bottom and sides

1. Start the potting process by watering the plant at least one 1 hour in advance.

2. Place a thin layer of gravel in the bottom of the container. Gravel placed at the bottom of a pot improves drainage and aeration beneath the soil. Keep in mind that too much gravel will reduce the growing area for the roots. Note well that some pots for plants are manufactured with drain holes, while others may have a plug in the drain hole or no drain hole at all. Ensure that the drain holes are open.

3. Place new compost made up of pliable, rich ingredients in pots.

4. Gently remove the plant from the container by turning it up side down in the palm of your hand allowing the stem to pass between your fingers.

5. Squeeze the pot from the bottom and sides or run a knife around the soil's edges to free the plant and its soil rather than pulling or tugging the plant from the top. If there are roots protruding from the drainage holes gently pinch or clip these off to make removal of the plant easier.

6. Ensure that the newly potted plant is not planted deeper than it was in the original pot. Set the plant ball about the same depth as it grew in the original container. One of the main causes of plant collapse and demise is planting too deep.

7. Fill around the ball with damp compost.

8. Firm the compost with the fingers, add more until it levels with the base of the stem.

9. Add a thin layer of mulch, but do not pile soil or mulch up around the main stem.

10. Water thoroughly and keep shaded for a week. Mist leaves daily to avoid wilting.

11. Do not fertilize newly potted plants in a hurry. Allow 4-6 weeks of settling in order to reduce the chances of burning the new root growth.

USE POTTED PLANTS TO YOUR ADVANTAGE

- *Flexibility:* Rearrange pots in accordance with occasion or the season, Add blooms or foliage to containers for a quick fix or to combine your favourites in one pot. Move the plants around.

- *Appearance:* Change the colour scheme. Groom the plants. Frame the doorway with pots. Encase the play area with hanging baskets. Large, rustic pots suggest years of growth; use them to brighten shady areas. Mask dilapidated eyesore with large pots filled with blooms.

- *Mobility:* Potted plants can be moved to a more suitable, sunny or shady location. Place these outside for a while to enjoy the night dew, the light rainfall and the morning sunlight.

- *Versatility:* Container gardens can be cultivated on a balcony, patio, in the courtyard or indoors. Place them on windowsills, decks or on the rooftop. Place them in doorways, on porches, in passages and on countertops. Display them on shelves, on sideboards or hang them from walls.
Variety: Grow plants of different characteristics and requirements next to each other. Collect and mass them. A jumble of pots lend a pleasant look. A trio of large pots make a garden seem settled.

- *Accessibility*: Containers are accessible to everyone; children, and those with impaired mobility.

- *No weeding*: Due to the small surface area it is unlikely that weeds will grow in these pots.

- *Limited garden tools* : Lightweight hand tools will do the easy maintenance job.

- *Control space invaders*: Use containers to control rampant growers. The container can be planted in the ground with the lip of the pot set even or a few inches above the soil surface.

- *Pest control*: If pests infected treat without disturbing the other healthy plants.

- *Garden on wheels*: Travel with your potted plants.

- *For commerce*: Suitable for wayside marketing delivery.

Group Potted Plants and
Enhance the Exterior

Display Your Potted Plants

You are the proud owner of those plants, showcase them! It could be a single pot or a sprawling garden of containers displaying a wealth of assorted textures, exhaling nose-tingling fragrances and showcasing a hype of radiant colours. Show them off. The plants enjoy the exaggerated publicity and are kept lively by the movement. Place the containers farther apart; up, down, to the front, to the rear so as to create a display that is always evolving. Make excellent additions to your containers, raise their beauty to new heights and simply set your plants on stage.

Stage your display as a single item, in small or large groupings and camouflage the landscape with a multitude of pots. Accompany the exhibits with garden ornaments, baskets, water features, wall plaques, household crockery, mobiles and sculptures. Combine containers and create display designs that would not have been possible otherwise. Display them atop handsome empty pots, attach them to sculptured drift wood and lay them beside garden art pieces. You may rearrange the displays throughout the seasons.

A bouncing display of Orchid blooms adding colour and zest to the landscape

As a Focal Point

A focal point brings an item into focus and will guide viewers to instantly know where to focus their attention. Anything that offers interest through size, shape or colour will serve as a focal point. Look around for objects of interest then find a place to put them. Focal points should look like they have always been a part of a garden and should seem comfortable in their surroundings.

Stage in Positions of Prominence

Stage your big-leaf plants to a position of prominence. They can be stunning on their own, can be displayed with elongated leaves or they can be pepped up with a backdrop. Small, slow growing plants as well as plants that display flowers with strong visual appeal or fragrance can also benefit from staging. Do so by bringing them closer to eye level.

Staging can also be an effective way to photograph beautiful plants with beautiful people. Staging creates the environment for exciting photographic displays. Include garden ornaments, seashells, driftwood or handsome empty pots. The options are numerous. Even the plants are elated and so they exhibit their brightest colour and their best poseur.

Creative Props

By placing pots atop of each other you can create compelling combinations and a measure of sophistication that would not have been possible with plants grown in the ground.

Overturned pots, kegs, reels, chairs, chunks of wood can do the trick. Use piles of bricks, building blocks and tree stumps to give plants and garden ornaments a boost. Raise them on shelves too.

Be an illusionist, hide the support behind a rank of containers and give those plants an elevated sensation. For plant stands that will be visible, options include attractive concrete, ceramic, wooden or metal support. Wooden supports seem best in their natural form.

Hang Them

Hanging baskets prefer some shade. Hang them on trees, on the balcony, in the greenhouse and in the interior of the dwelling house. Complete the arbour or the gazebo with a rich display of baskets, overflowing with greenery or blooms.

In Hallow Tree Trunks

Don't be daunted by the heaviness of these tree trunks often see lain idly by the wayside.

Impossible to lift? Roll them. Motivated by a picture in the Jamaican Health, Home and Garden Magazine my enthusiastic gardening friend fell a palm tree. She drastically increased her stock of containers. Yet another gardening spectacular.

TRICKS FOR SUCCESSFUL CONTAINER GARDENING

Mulching Matters Some potted plants, especially those with a single upright stem, reveal a great deal of soil. Brighten up the boring soil with a layer of glass marbles, painted snail shells, river stones, terra-cotta pebbles or wood chips. Keep the mulch away from the plant stems to allow proper ventilation.

Create A Garden Sculpture Select a container with low growing plants. Place an intricate obelisk or sculptural looking object beside it. This is your garden sculpture.

Fill All The Space Plant generously and closely, and give your container a full and finished look. Squeeze root balls into narrow shapes and make space for other plants. Watering, feeding and grooming will keep your display in top shape.

Boost Them Up Boost up floral arrangements, potted plants and containers by sticking in little vials and smaller pots with bright, fresh flowers. Add crystal or china. Throw on a table-runner, place an empty vase, driftwood, an interesting basket, a book or a big platter beside the container.

Lift Them Up You will need two pots; one a little bigger than the other. Put soil in the bigger pot, leaving about 2 in. at the top. Sit the smaller container in the centre and fill with soil. Put plants in both containers. Plant the taller plants in the smaller container to give the height you want. For the bigger pot you will select plants that will grow up to camouflage and hug the smaller pot.

Set The Stage When grouping assorted containers raise a few in the back. Achieve this by placing them on bricks, on chunks of wood or on up-sided down pots. Place the taller ones and those with broad leaves at the back.

***A* Fancy Container, A Simple Plant** If you are using a fancy container, you should use a simple plant. This design is more eye-catching and will eliminate confusion to the eyes.

Foliage Only The colours, shapes, textures, sizes of foliage are overwhelming. Group assorted green foliage or coloured foliage

only and you will be amazed at the multitude of natural tones, textures, shades and hues.

Highlight With Ground Cover Place one or two large containers in a bed of ground cover. This will inject a punch of colour and flair. Some ground covers may attempt to creep up the sides of the container and settle their roots in the pots too. Soon there will be a happy mix of plants exhibiting shades of assorted colours.

Keep Your Garden Fresh No plant can continue blooming forever. When the blooms fade remove them from your collection and replace these from your 'stand by' plants. Remove the pups, the daughters, the suckers and repot the many new plants.

Multiply Your Stock Keep some small pots, a portion of suitable soil and some gravel handy. As you prune you may 'stick' a few selected stems or suckers in a pot. Drop a few seeds in some pots and cover with a thin layer of soil. Before long you will have an amazing collection of new plants and fresh seedlings. Share these with your garden visitors.

Add Some Frills For a softer, more natural look, add a sprig or two of trailing plants to your containers. Some of these trailing plants even bloom and will add more

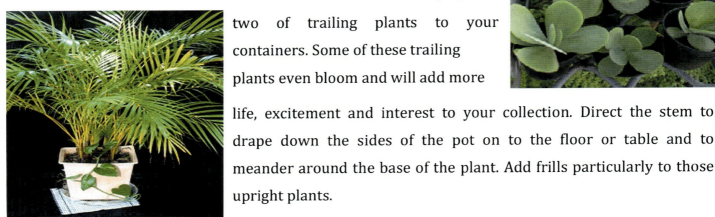

life, excitement and interest to your collection. Direct the stem to drape down the sides of the pot on to the floor or table and to meander around the base of the plant. Add frills particularly to those upright plants.

This large-type plant has been restricted to its container for many years

Restrict Their Growth Containers restrict the growth and size of plants which often results in the development of a partial Bonsai. We unknowingly create this art form by keeping the plant confined to a pot and often the result is altogether pleasing.

Group Them Plants show off to a better advantage if they are planted or displayed in multiples. One or two will look great for large specimens but very often a group of three will create a much more effective display. Together they will create a unified mass instead of looking like lonesome polka dots.

Plants do enhance the beauty of each other. Be reminded to take into account the basic needs of each plant, especially when planting them together in one container or in one bed. Ensure their compatibility. Grouping makes allowance for interchanging, alterations and for intended colour scheme.

A Royal Palm restricted in a pot for 10 years while its counterparts tower 50 ft. high

GARDENING PASSION

Romance In The Garden

Plant two or three plants in one pot; you will be flabbergasted at the love affair that takes place there

Blooms of the Shampoo Ginger entwined with the foliage of the Zebra plant

The Canna Lily unfolds its attractive blooms that intimately engage the neighbouring Palm

The Rubber Plant and the Palm share a loving relationship

Is that a bloom of the croton? No, the Ixora is just being a romantic neighbour

GARDENING PASSION

CONTAINERS DAZZLING DELGHTS

Dahlias

Dahlias; a large annual.

The showy Dahlias come in various sizes and shapes and in all colours except blue. Propagation is usually by seeds, but tubers are easier and faster to grow. Plant them individually or in small clumps. Set the tubers with the eyes pointing up and cover with about 2 in. soil. Dahlias require full sun, fertile and well drained soil. Avoid setting up tubers during rainy months because prolonged moisture induces rotting. Add organic matter to improve fertility. Dahlias will start flowering about 8-10 weeks after planting. A little shade during the mid-day sun provides beneficial protection from the excessive heat. They also need protection from the wind. Flowering stops if growth is retarded by drought or insufficient nutrients. Plant dwarf Dahlias as bedding, borders and edging plants. They are extremely beautiful in containers. Use the taller cultivars in borders or in the centre of round gardens.

The Crown of Thorns, Christ Plant, Crucifixion Plant

It is appropriate to classify the Crown of Thorns; Euphorbia milii, as a container's delight, as with the right conditions it will supply and maintain blooms all year round. It is a hardy, drought tolerant, semi-succulent shrub covered in strong thorns. The length of the blooming season depends on the light intensity. The blooming season runs from early spring to mid-summer. The showy bracts are available in red, salmon, yellow, orange and white. Crown of Thorns welcome some misting during the hot summer months. Leaves grow only on new growth and will not be replaced when they fall.

Crown of Thorns will tolerate much pruning which will help to retain the overall shape of the plant and will encourage bushiness. Being a slow growing plant it should be pruned every 2-3 years. Prune during the spring which has cool, dry weather to lessen the risk of stem disease. Remove 1/3rd up to 2/3rds of growth. Select the longest branches and cut back to a lateral branch on the interior of the plant. Ensure that the plant gets a lot of light after cutting back so the new growth stays stocky and compact. Prune by using a clean, sharp knife, not secateurs, to cut off the branch at the point where it meets the mother stem. Wear gloves when pruning or taking cuttings. Wash thoroughly afterwards as the sap is poisonous and will irritate the skin. The slim-line flower stalks carry a sticky substance that can get on the fingers when you groom the plant. Stop the flow of sap by dipping the end in water. Use cuttings to propagate new plants.

Place cuttings in a dry and well ventilated area. Let them stand for a day or two to allow the cut to harden and to form a callus. Dip the end into rooting hormone then set these new cuttings in pots or plant nursery bags with moist, sandy compost. If the medium stays too wet the cuttings will rot. Adequate drainage is vital for all plants especially those grown in containers. Place these nursery plants in a warm bright spot. Roots will be established within 4-6 weeks. Allow the top of the soil to dry before watering but never allow the roots to dry out completely. Overwatering will cause loss of leaves. Adequate water during the dry season will coax the plant to bloom.

These plants will cope with some neglect and will stand up to almost any weather conditions. They are tolerant of salty soils. Fertilize once per month with half strength foliar fertilizer. Crown of Thorns do look stunning in the garden and very nice in coloured pots but if you display them in white pots you will be bewildered at the very pleasing result. Use you collection to line your sunny walkway, to transfer to and enhance the interior of your house or as a focal point in the landscape. Crown of Thorns and other succulents are ideal for the rock gardens. Because of the thorns they are not suitable for young gardeners. Do not plant the crown of thorns next to a fish pond.

Crown Of Thorns in the Garden

E. milii "Lila"

E .milii " Doung Isree "

E. milii "Mini Belle "

E. milii " Milii Dinni "

E. milii "Minoche"

E .milii "Dwarf Apache"

E. milii "Tickled Pink"

E. milii "Virginia"

E. milii "Coral"

E. milii "Primrose Yellow"

E. milii " Zeus Crown "

E. milii "Red Princess"

GARDENING PASSION

A CONTAINER'S DELIGHT

E. milii "Primrose Yellow"

CHAPTER FOUR
ELEGANT GARDENS

"Every garden is unique with a multitude of choices in soils, plants and theme. Finding your garden theme is as best as seeing what brings a smile to your face."
Anonymous

A garden is a piece of land selected for the cultivation of flowers, fruits or vegetables. It consists of a collection of natural elements. A garden is exposed to open air in order to complete the natural aesthetics. The natural elements are purposely arranged thus engaging all the senses and creating an environment for the viewer to experience and appreciate. A garden exceeds the experience of both space and time and is designed for functional purposes as well as for emotional satisfaction. Enclosed plants such as those in greenhouses or conservatories form a different category. Gardens can be made in containers, on rooftops and on windowsills. It gloriously brings us in touch with nature.

A 'posh' garden; elegantly portrayed with potted Crown of Thorns and manicured Duranta Gold

RAISED GARDENS

Raised bed gardening is an old gardening practice which offers several advantages compared to growing plants on the level ground. It is gardening in soil that has been mounded or contained higher than the surrounding level. Bringing the garden closer to the gardener is one idea behind the raised garden. Those who do not have the required space to plant a traditional garden often design an elevated garden.

A raised garden fully utilized; growing cuttings from the Duranta Gold

This gardening technique is best utilized in areas with poor drainage, surplus stones, poor soil quality or uneven ground surface. This technique puts an end to the grief of those ardent gardeners who experience physical impairment as they will not have the need to employ the back breaking effort needed for spadework and heavy duty tools. Raised gardens create a "level playfield" where both the novice and the experienced gardener can practice their skills and use this technique to break the monotony of the landscape. A raised bed allows one to bring in the best soil which never gets compacted and the extra height allows the garden bed to warm up quickly. It is a convenient and low-maintenance method of growing flowers and vegetables in small spaces. Create a raised bed by simply piling the soil. However, if you require something higher or more permanent, you will want to frame your raised bed. Make your gardens in multiple boxes, these can be placed in different locations around the landscape. These boxes are also beautiful and they make stylish additions to any landscaping design.

Tips For Raised Gardens

The design employed for the raised garden will depend on the available space, terrain and the planting goals. Whatever the design, its location should add interest to the space.

1. Be realistic, start small and build on the project as you go along. **2.** The garden is best when placed in good view from the porch or patio. **3.** Use them to define walkways or driveways. **4.** Place beds away from the busy walk way to save anyone stumbling over them. **5.** Place them in open space and not around corners. **6.** Place them alongside the fence or under tall trees. **7.** Place them around large tree stumps or boulders.

Advantages of The Raised Gardens

- **Soil Control:** Having selected the best soil there is no need to till. The soil will remain light and aerated and will not get compacted from being trampled.

- **Use of Maximum Space:** These gardens do not require the usual space between rows. They ensure the use of every inch of garden space.

- **Higher Yields:** All space is used and best practices will result in higher yields.

- **Best Drainage:** These elevated beds drain more rapidly than gardens at ground level. They are also usually easier to water. The size makes it perfect for the installation of drip irrigation.

- **Controlling Animals and Pests:** Strayed animals, birds or pets may try gain easy access to these gardens. Keep pests away by spraying the perimeter of the bed. Cover with a mesh or netting. **Easy On The Back:** Raised gardens are often "stoop" free. The ideal height of 36 in.

- **Early Start:** Raised beds are a great way to quickly start your garden, as these are even warmer than gardens at ground level. They are also less prone to weeds.

Tending Raised Gardens

1. Install an irrigation system and water regularly. **2.** Install a barrier to roots and weeds.

3. Mulch after planting. **4.** Top dress annually with compost. **5.** Fluff the soil occasionally.

6. Cover up the soil, even when you are not gardening, a thin layer of mulch will do.

7. Plant annuals or quick crops and plant ahead to extend the season. **8.** Avoid walking in the garden as trampling will compact the soil. **9.** Do some composting directly in your elevated garden.

FRAMED GARDEN BED

A framed garden bed is likened to a large, shallow container. Frame the garden with stones, bricks or concrete building blocks, these are inexpensive and they last forever. Put extra soil in the holes of the blocks and plant small decorative plants or herbs in them. Build a four-sided frame, approximately 1-2 ft. in height and place in a designated area. Frames may be as long as desired but 4 ft. in width is comfortable as this allows free access to the middle of the bed. Geometrically designed beds placed beside each other will enhance the landscape. Ensure easy access to water or install an irrigation system.

Add a layer of pebbles and coarse sand along the floor of the bed to facilitate drainage. Fill the bed with light, rich humus that is rid of weeds and stones. Sow the seeds or plant the seedlings. Add 2 in. of mulch. Group together plants of similar nutrient, water and sunlight requirements. You may also enhance your framed garden by adding low picket fencing or by placing a number of small potted plants around the frame.

Frame the space

CONTAINER GARDENS

Container gardens can be cultivated in large or small pots, or in boxes and placed at different locations. Extra large or heavy pots can be moved around on castors. Other large containers may be permanently placed and can look more intriguing when finishing touches are added. Rosette plants and low growing ground covers make superb accessories. These containers should not be forced to stand on their own. They look better in the company of other assorted pots, over hanging trees or controllable decorative vines.

MOUND GARDENING

Mound gardening can be done on the spot of your choice. Identify the area, till the soil and incorporate 18 in. of rich topsoil to create the mound. The shape and the size of the mound will be determined by the presence of other garden features, the purpose of the bed, the style and the available space. With time, this mound will be flattened. That should not happen too fast if the border is re-enforced. Padding the borders with stones, bricks or bits of wood will do the trick. The gardening secret is that you cover the material used to re-enforce the borders. Maintain the mound by adding more soil. Ensure that the bed is accessible from all sides. Circle-weed to highlight the design.

Plant in containers and place them in areas of your choice

Incorporate some rich soil and create a Mound garden around the base of trees

WATER GARDENS

Introduce water gardens and add a touch of serenity, colour and movement to your landscape. There is nothing that can beautify your landscape faster than a water garden, inhabited by colourful fish, aquatic plants and completed with a border of exotic vegetation. Water contained in any form, shape or size, placed outside and complemented by other features is a thing of sheer beauty. The flickering reflections of the sun, the ripples encouraged by the soft wind and the reflection of waving leaves are a welcome presence in any garden. Dressing up the

Utilize the water garden and create the ideal home for aquatic plants and animals

container with water plants transforms the display to a whole new dimension. This creates compositions that are vibrant and dynamic, especially when contrasting shapes, colours and forms are used. A water garden allows you to grow plants that do not thrive in any other environment.

There are two kinds of water gardens, the still and the active. You can garden in the former but not the latter. Most aquatic plants and animals do prefer the still garden. Gardening in water may seem odd as all the rules and garden wisdom get turned up-side down. For instance, you no longer need to ensure fast-draining soil and you can successfully pot plants in the heaviest clay soil.

Any container that is capable of holding water qualifies as a pond. A water garden is an ecological system. It should be exposed to 5-6 hours of sun per day, as this is the ideal requirement of the animals and plants involved. Too much sun will increase the growth of algae. It is best to select a semi-shaded area. For security reasons the water garden should not be deeper than 18 in.

Build A Water Garden

- Select a suitable spot and dig a hole to accommodate the container or pond liner.

- Fit the container in the hole leaving the lid about 12 in. above ground level.

- Place river stones at the bottom of the container.

Group assorted aquatic plants in mesh baskets

- Add clean water and allow the water to stand for 2-3 days.

- Plant the aquatic plants in mesh baskets.

- Add animal life; fish and snails. Feed them as directed. Look out for the ravenous water bird as he can certainly have all his fishy meals there.

Planting the Aquatic Garden

Introduce aquatic plants by planting them in plastic or mesh baskets, then rest them on the floor of the pond. The look is very natural and these baskets can be easily removed for maintenance. Groom plants by removing decaying leaves and dead roots. These will rot in the substrate and build up sludge on the floor. Add these roots and leaves to the compost heap. Repot once every two years. Some of these plants produce runners; so separate the young shoots from the mother or parent plant. Camouflage or soften the hard edge of the container by training a cascading plant such as the water mint (*Mentha aquatica*), with its fragrant leaves and powder-blue flowers. Aim for a plant and container combination that is harmonious and proportionate. Keep this garden simple.

Water Lettuce and blooming Water Hyacinth

Four Water Gardening Rules

1. Cultivate aquatic plants, breed fish and water snails for ecological balance. **2.** Grow aquatic plants in their own pots or mesh baskets. **3.** Keep 75 % of the water surface covered with vegetation. The surface may vary with the type of fish involved. 4. There is no need to change the water but you should top it up every few days to replace the water that may have evaporated.

Water Snails in the Garden

Water snails are scavengers, they eat algae, mostly the ones on the pond surface. They do not crawl out of the pond, neither do they eat the decorative plants. They lay their eggs on the underside of the leaves of the water lilies. Do not throw them out when you repot. Ensure preservation of the invaluable animal life.

Understanding the problematic Algae

Algae are ubiquitous, non–flowering plant forms that are an unavoidable and a recurring part of pond keeping. It is a problem that occurs with most new ponds and keeping it under control requires proper maintenance. The main cause is that there are decaying materials that release nitrates and phosphates and this promotes the growth of algae. Even as plants become established, if they are not of the type that use up nitrates and phosphates quicker than algae, there will be a lot of algae present. As the pond gets older the growth goes into decline. Minimize the growth of algae by:

1. Ensuring that there is no water run-off into the pond.

2. Maintaining the pond by removing the sludge.

3. Not over feeding the fish or water snails.

4. Not overloading the pond with fish.

5. Avoiding the use of rich soil to pot those plants; instead use clay or loamy soil.

6. Avoiding the use of fertilizers.

7. Put in some underwater or submerged aquatic plants to mop up nutrients and release oxygen during the day. This oxygen sustains the animal life in the pond.

Those Annoying Mosquitoes The water garden should not be a breeding ground for mosquitoes. Any thing that looks like an ideal nursery for the mosquitoes must be properly maintained. Do not let mosquitoes ruin your garden pleasures; plant a Neem tree. (Mosquito tree)

- Plant some garlic vines; mosquitoes detest the smell of garlic.
- Mow the lawn weekly as mosquitoes hide in tall grasses.
- Plant original Marigold as these produce a pungent odour that mosquitoes detest.
- Ensure that fish are in the water garden. The **Guppy** fish locally called 'groupie' also eat the mosquito larvae.

The Friendly Toad

Thanks for the photograph

The toad can catch and eat four hundred mosquitoes in one night; allow it to stay. The female however, may deposit thousands of unwelcome croaking residents. The tadpoles are herbaceous and consume algae.

THE HERB GARDEN

Herbs, rich in legends are medicinal, culinary and ornamental plants that have been used since man's earliest days on earth. Herbalists prescribe and supply natural medications derived from these herbs. Herbs are known for their scented oils that are used in fragrances, cosmetics and medicines. The oils derived from herbs contain Vitamin E and other minerals and are loaded with antioxidants. Herbs are easy to grow, require minimum maintenance and are adaptable to a variety of soils. When planting a herb garden identify a convenient spot that is easily accessible to the kitchen. This will render it quite easy to step out and reach for the herbs to add flavour to the soup, brew some tea or to season the meats and pep up the punch. Most herbs are associated with certain dishes and can transform your simple meal into a tantalizing explosion of taste and pleasant smell.

Enhance your meals with herbs by adding sprigs of coarser herbs to the glowing coals on the barbeque or to the hot water tray in the oven. This will give meats, stews and soups an aromatic seasoned flavour. Herbs supply natural flavours that eliminate the need for salt and other condiments.

Planting Herbs

A basic herb garden contains a combination of Mints, Basil, Parsley, Sage, Lemon Grass, Aloe Vera, White Periwinkle, Fever grass, Thyme and Rosemary. One may be also expected to plant Worm grass, Dandelion, Spirit weed, Kola nut and Physic nut. Propagate many herbs from cuttings taken in spring. Cuttings with flowers forming on them are not likely to root strongly so cut the flowers off. Plants that have been heavily fertilized to stimulate lush growth produce poor cuttings. Water plants well, at least 12 hours before you take cuttings. The roots of newly planted herbs will be formed within 2 - 6 weeks or longer. Water generously until the plants are well established. Plants with thin leaves require more water during the dry season.

Some herbs are rampant growers. Control them by planting in large plastic pots with the bottom removed and the top rim emerging 2 in. above the soil surface. Cut back sprouts for tea or garnish. Pinch back to keep them from blooming, to provide sprigs and to inspire bushier growth. Some herbs such as the Sage and Mints masquerade as perennials because they can be used for decorating, fragrance or for cuisine. Plant a 'herb pot' and provide lots of exciting plants to create a very manageable green space for the patio or a small garden.

Soil Preference

Herbs grown in soil that is too rich tend to be lanky and inferior in flavour and colour. Amend the soil with leaf mould or compost and add organic matter to improve drainage. Herbs are at their best in well drained soil. Do not add fertilizer. Choose an accessible spot in the landscape that gets at least 6 hours of sunlight and is away from shade-casting buildings and trees.

Harvest and Store Herbs

Herbs are at the peak of intensity in their flavour and fragrance just before flowering as their flavouring oils have also peaked. Reap herbs early in the morning when

Aloe Vera (Sinkle Bible)

their aromas are at their highest levels. When harvesting, make cuts that will improve the shape of the plant. Bundle 5 or 6 stems and hang these up side down in a warm dry place. Herbs can also be dried in the microwave or in the oven. Store dried herbs in brown paper bags. Sweetly fragrant herbs are wonderful for teas and for potpourri. For culinary herbs freezing is an option. Select and wash the best quality herbs, pat the leaves with a paper towel until dry. Wrap single portions in freezer paper or place in zip lock bags, seal and freeze. These will not be suitable for garnish as they will become limp when thawed. Instead they can be chopped and used in cooking. Use within 2 months. Some herbs do not retain as much flavour when preserved by any method and should only be used when fresh.

Some Common Uses of Herbs

- Use the sweet smelling herbs as fillers in floral or fruit arrangements.

- Use herbs to add aroma to the surroundings.

- Use fragrant herbs in potpourri to infuse intriguing aromas.

- Use culinary herbs in combination with dried spices.

A cup of herb tea

- Use herbs in jams, marmalades, syrups, hot or cold beverage and in chutneys.

- Use herbs in crafts such as greeting cards, wall pictures, sachets and hanging decorations.

- Use aromatic herbs in paper making projects.

Sprigs of the Rosemary

GARDENING PASSION

Some Benefits of Medicinal Herbs

Studies have shown that herbs offer a wide range of health benefits. It involves the use of leaves, seeds, bark, berries, nuts, rhizomes, fruits, roots and flowers and can be found among some popular herbs such as ; Cymbopogan citrates (Lemon Grass), Mentha x gentilis (Black Mint), (Scotch mint), Peppermint and Cerasee.

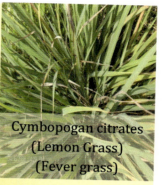

Cymbopogan citrates
(Lemon Grass)
(Fever grass)

- Some herb teas have a natural diuretic effect;, they help to remove excess water from the body.

- Some herbs increase the flow of bile which is essential for digestion.

- Some are rich in chlorine, this prevents and treats a fatty liver.

Mentha x gentilis (Black Mint)

- Herbs also help to cure hepatitis.

- The tea and juice of some herbs can help lower serum cholesterol and uric acid levels.

- Some herbs are blood cleansers and help prevent age spots and other skin disorders.

- Some herbs are used as a mild laxative in habitual constipation.

- Some herbs are good for fever, stress and insomnia.

Cerasee, with
pods and seeds

- The root tea of herbs combined with a good diet and exercise can eliminate diabetes.

- Some herbs relieve menopausal symptoms.

- Some herbs are a source of organic magnesium and contribute to bone density and dental health.

- Some herbs are rich in iron content.

ROCK GARDENS

The rock garden, also known as a rockery, is a fascinating sub-group of the horticultural arts. It is not a haphazard stockpile of rocks with lichens on their craggy surfaces, but a garden esthetically arranged with porous rocks, evergreens and mosses. It adds interest and visual appeal and is often made to integrate slopes in the landscape or on hard to manage areas. It is a departure from the traditional flowerbed design and can be used to stimulate the feeling of a rugged terrain. Keen attention should be paid to the principles of design which includes colour, texture, height and shape. A good design of a rock garden requires careful selection of stones, plants and appropriate accessories. Plants are not limited to those that naturally grow among rocks, like the cactus and succulents. Selected plants that exhibit variations of height and texture. Low growing perennials hardy plants that will add colour can be included. Add suitable garden ornaments.

Work with a design in mind. Start by setting the rocks in the front part of the garden then work your way upward. Leave a few pockets of different sizes between rocks for the plants. After planting, top dress the surface with gravel or small stones. Add mosses and trailing Ivy that will spill over to soften the area. The sparsely planted rock garden requires little care. Just a little fertilizer, pruning and weeding will do.

Build A Rock Garden

- If necessary rid the spot of stones, grass, weeds and shrubs.
- Cover the ground with textile or plastic ground cover available in the garden supply outlets. Use
- layers of newspaper, sheets of plastic or tarpaulin. This covering will prevent grass from growing up.
- Select one geological type of rocks of varying sizes.
- Mass rocks unevenly. Use the smaller ones to disguise the ground cover.
- Add 12 in. rich soil between rocks.
- Select suitable plants that will survive the climatic conditions.
- Add suitable potted plants, disguising the pots with stones. Group plants with similar growing requirements.
- Water features like ponds can be incorporated. A container with water can do the trick.
- Include a dry streambed with a ribbon of smooth stones or a row of sand and pebbles. Be creative. Add a dry tree trunk, an interesting limb or a piece of driftwood.

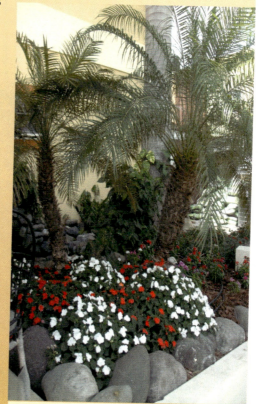

A brightly coloured Rock Garden

GARDENING PASSION

M I X E D   G A R D E N S

A spectacular display in the mixed garden. dappled shade provided by the over hanging trees. The morning sun trickles in from behind giving a soft sheen white blooms

The mixed garden which is a combination of a variety of plants such as trees, shrubs, perennials, annuals, herbs and grasses is usually laid out in a 'hodge-podge' design. There is also the presence of assorted foliage, ornamentals, climbers and bulbs. These mixed gardens evolve as a result of gardeners collecting assorted plants and planting them in the available space. This wide selection of plants allows for a combination of variety of garden features and styles. In a mixed garden you will find a little of everything. There you are likely to find lots of gardening blunders, planting drama, plant competition, all coming together in a very irregular yet often pleasing and delightful setting..

Adding Interest and Drama

Extra large pots are often included to add drama and impact and to integrate the architecture with the landscape. Mixed gardens create interest and allow your garden to function all year round. The individual characteristics of plants, their aroma and the assortment of colours all contribute to a dynamic scene.

Large pots add drama and impact.

Art Forms Amidst the Garden

A mixed garden is comprised of a wide variety of creative art forms such as the Bonsai and Topiary. Accessories are bountiful. Natural or man-made shades are installed and seats are strategically placed. Colourful gazebos, eye-catching lawn umbrellas, connecting bridges, electrical or solar lighting and anything that will enhance the general beauty. Paved walkways are made to accommodate two, walking side by side.

A bonsai-like art form

Wild life abounds here

Make space for the biting ants, the frightened crabs, the friendly lizards and do not get caught in the nettled spider webs. The assorted species of birds; the heron, the long-legged wading bird, the bright-eyed hawk, the screeching owls are all intimately attracted to the colours, the moving water, the aroma and the fruity trees. They all converge and liven up what would have been a quiet garden into a busy and buzzing haven, adding life, colour and excitement to a prolific gardening affair.

After a shower of rain this 'garden pet' basked in full view and posed for this picture

Changeable foliage colours

Overcome the Challenges

Areas of light and shade provide the right environment in which to grow sun and shade loving plants. The mixed garden is diverse and is able to cope with any gardening challenge encountered. This being so, we find that the dry shade, the dry soil, the wet area, the stony patch and even the unsightly corner can all be successfully integrated into the mixed garden.

Blooms and Colours In this grand mix you will find those ever-blooming annuals, the exotic and powerful perennials and the blazingly bright coloured tropical plants. The mixed garden is never without blooms. It is generously endowed with a variety of flower types that bloom at different times of the gardener's calendar and is always ready to lend that glowing spark on any given morning. Here you will find blooms and foliage that are ready

for the vase or will sit out there and brighten the garden.

These blooms not only bring an influx of colours and portray a warm welcome to the beautiful surroundings but they add captivating fragrances as well.

A spray of mauve

Vanda in bloom

Plants enjoy the company of each other

GARDENING PASSION

S H A D E G A R D E N

A collection plants in light or medium shade provided by overhanging trees

The shade garden is cultivated in the shade; under trees, in the greenhouse, on the patio or on the shady sides of buildings. It is usually an ornamental garden with a predominance of lush greens and possesses a natural, yet almost ethereal attractiveness. It offers the opportunity to collect and indulge in a whole new category of wonderful plants. A shaded location will keep the plants cooler.

Light Shade
Light shade may be an area that is completely shaded but brightly lit, or an area that enjoys filtered or dappled sunlight for long periods. Airy and lightly branched trees are typical for filtering sunlight. The colour of flowers and foliage is much more brilliant and the blooms last longer when shielded from the intense midday sun.

Partial or Medium Shade

Partial or medium shade is present when direct sunlight is blocked from an area for most of the day. Dappled sunlight is similar to partial shade. Partial shade is achieved when the sun filters its way through the branches of the trees. Many landscapes enjoy large or small areas of partial shade where sections of the yard are shaded by tall, spreading trees for most of the day but receive some direct sun early or late in the day.

I fancy the open plan and the dappled sunlight that spreading trees provide. This shade is economical and allows for the training of topiary and bonsai specimens. Gardening under a canopy of leaves, on a floor that is carpeted and decorated with a variety of textures gives a sheltered and comfortable feeling. The plants are dust free, require less grooming and require a minimal amount of weeding. Look out for snails and slugs; they often make the moist environment their preferred home.

Full or Dense Shade

Full or dense shade is created when no direct sunlight reaches the ground at any time of the day; it lasts all day. There are not many plants, except the mushrooms that can survive in total darkness. Lighten up full shade by removing tree branches. As trees and shrubs mature landscapes change their degree of shade so that the originally sunny garden may evolve into a shady one. Light patterns also change with the season, therefore an area that is in full sun in summer when the sun is high in the sky may have medium shade in spring and winter when the sun is at a lower angle. Observe the seasons and record the type of shade that is present.

Shade in the Greenhouse

The greenhouse accommodates extensive plant displays. The plants enjoy its shaded surroundings and the security of being protected from the onslaught of the wind, rain and sun. It is usually made of wood, fiberglass or transparent plastic with perforated walls which provide ample ventilation. Its floor is often covered with gravel, allowing for additional humidity. It is essential to have running water in close proximity as there will be the need to water plants regularly. Electricity can be an added feature to allow for night viewing or for a water feature.

Selecting Shade Loving Plants

Plants that usually produce brightly coloured blooms will produce less blooms when grown in the shade. As you design this garden you should rely more on attractive combinations and contrasting foliage, texture and plant forms, rather than on the blooms. Foliage can be used to add colour to the shade garden. White, yellow, striped and marbled leaves, or silvery-mottled leaves can brighten the shadiest spot. Glossy leaves have more impact in the shade than the dull or velvety ones. Variegated or yellow-green foliage is evident in the shade more than solid green or blue-green foliage. To highlight plants in the shade you should select plants with light-coloured blooms or silvery foliage.

Soil Requirements

Some shade gardens, though they enjoy cooler temperature tend to be quite dry. The addition of organic matter to the soil will help to keep some moisture in. Earthworms will incorporate surface applied organic matter, help loosen heavy clay soils and improve drainage. If the soil is sandy the organic matter will increase its water holding capacity as the organic material breaks down. Some shade tolerant plants will adapt to low moisture conditions while others require moist shade.

Challenges in the Shade

Not all plants are able to grow to their fullest or bloom profusely in the shade. It may then become necessary to increase the amount of dappled sunlight in a shaded garden. Strong winds can batter the plants and is also capable of drying out the limited moisture they receive. Poor air circulation may be caused from low-hanging branches or walls that block air movement. Insufficient air and lower light levels will cause the foliage to stay wet for longer periods in the shade than in sunny areas. Plant diseases are likely to develop under shaded conditions. Avoid this by raising plants to a higher level or by spacing them apart to allow better circulation of air.

CACTI AND SUCCULENTS GARDEN

The Cacti are some of nature's most exotic plants which are mistakenly seen as lonely, bland plants that grow only in the desert. Cacti come in many different shapes, sizes and colours and they produce beautiful flowers too. The Desert type requires lots of direct sunlight. The Shade or Tropical type thrives under conditions similar to other tropical plants. They require more nutrients and should be fertilized more regularly than sun loving cacti. Most succulents have a rosette shape and the leaves are tightly packed in order to conserve water.

Espostoa melanostele

Euphorbia acteal
(Elkon) (Frilled fan)

Euphorbia tirucalli
(Milk Bush) (Pencil Euphorbia)

Selenicereus anthonyanus
(Zig Zag Cactus)
(Fishbone cactus)

Opuntia microdasys
(Bunny Ears)

Lobivia hertrichiana
(Scarlet gob)

Rebutia miniscula
(Mexican Sun)

GARDENING PASSION

Cactus

The Cactus garden is most often designed on a slope, as this allows for proper drainage. Do not be deterred by the hairy, waxy skin and spines on most cacti, as you can use a metal or wooden tong to hold them. You can also fold layers of newspaper into a strip about 1in. wide and long enough to wrap around the cactus. Leave two tails to grab as a handle for moving the plant around. Plant them in regular planting medium with equal amount of topsoil and coarse sand. Other poor mixtures of soil will retard their growth. Their root systems are frail and cannot cope with the tough,

Gorgeous blooms; a velvety touch

clay soil types. When planting the rosette shaped types remove the few lower leaves. Plant the leaves you have removed in a well lit, but shaded spot and wait for new plantlets. Cacti are tough, but if neglected or put into the wrong environment they will decline or even die just like any other plant. Cacti will not show early signs of stress like wilting, yellow or falling leaves but will look unaffected until it is sometimes too late for plant surgery or the application of any other remedy.

Potting Cacti

- Choose either an ornamental or a neutral container with adequate drainage holes.

- Place shards or pebbles over the drainage holes to prevent the soil from draining out.

- Fill the pot with prepared soil to 1/3rd its capacity.

- Remove shoots by gently twisting them off. Use gloves, tongs or a paper .

- Add a layer of coarse sand.   Use a pencil size stick to make a hole in the soil.

- Plant but do not bury the body of the cactus. Allow the soil to dry between watering. To add interest, decorate with coloured pebbles, shells, marbles or small bits of bevelled mirror.

THE DRAMATIC CANNA LILY

Canna x generalis The Canna Lily is a vigorous tropical and perennial plant with thick rhizomes and large, green, paddle-shaped leaves approximately 2 ft. long and 1 ft. wide. In recent years cultivars with handsome yellow stripes, bronze-purple or variegated leaves have been developed. The Cannas carry long, erect stems topped with magnificent clusters of red, orange-red, yellow, hot pink or apricot flowers. Large gladiolus-like, fragrance-free blooms appear all year round.

Growing Canna Lily Most Canna Lily varieties grow to a height of 3-5 ft. but a few towering "giants" may reach 8-10 ft. Smaller "dwarf" varieties that grow only 1 1/2-2 ft. tall are suitable for containers. The plants are fast growing and easy to please. They produce a good show even in areas with short growing seasons. Canna indica is commonly known as Indian Shot because of its hard, black, pea-like seeds used in games.

They are also used as mosaic material in craft. Dividing the rhizomes is the easiest way to reproduce Canna Lily. Some dwarf cultivars can be grown from seeds.

C. Lily 'Tropical sunrise'

C. Lily 'The President'

C. Lily 'Tropicanna'

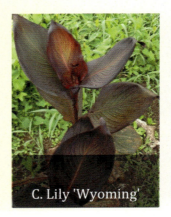
C. Lily 'Wyoming'

C .Lily 'Cleopatra'

Sun and Soil
The Canna Lily will grow best in full sun but will thrive in partial shade. They fancy well drained, evenly moist, rich, sandy soil that is free of grass and weeds. Canna Lily is a heavy feeder and thrives in rich organic matter. For the promotion of lush growth, amend the soil with lots of compost and add a balanced slow-release fertilizer. The most beautiful bloom I have seen was from a plant that grew in an old compost heap. That guided me to add another inch of compost to the bed. Canna Lily grows from rhizomes that extend beyond the confines of the garden. The thick branching rhizome is quite busy underground seeking new places to send up new suckers. Set rhizomes with their growing tip up and just deep enough so that they are barely covered. Remove flowers and dry leaves as they fade; this will encourage new and vibrant blooms. Once the plant has stopped producing new blooms it should be discarded, by cutting above the base of the plant.

Landscape Uses
The Canna Lilies are among the plants that offer long-lasting colours all year round and that is the number one reason they find themselves in municipal plantings. They add dramatic colours and a tropical flair to road median strips, parks, airports, shopping centres and other public areas. Plant your Canna Lilies in small groupings and in large pots or tuck them between small to medium shrubs. They need little maintenance. Canna Lilies harmonize well and can be used successfully in mixed borders and mound beds. Their rich, pronounceable colours, varied height and assorted foliage make them an excellent choice to brighten any sunny spot in the landscape. Any of these varieties can be used as temporary screens, accents or background plantings. Canna Lilies attract hummingbirds while butterflies find it a pleasure to lay their eggs on the underside of the leaves. The development process of a new set of butterflies begins and ends right there in the garden. The leaves are eaten by the caterpillars and while this can be a little unsightly, the beautiful butterflies that emerge after a few weeks do compensate for the minor damages. Expect the horrible slugs that regard these soft, juicy leaves as their most scrumptious meal. Look for them as they come out for food at nightfall.

THE VEGETABLE PATCH

Pumpkin blooms

Sure, you love flowers and it may seem difficult to resist the temptation to cover every square inch of land space with beds of flowering plants. You will however, find equal pleasure in the vegetable patch. Here you may cultivate lots of tomatoes, pumpkins, carrots, onions, peppers, okras and beans. This garden supplies food to which there is no comparison to the high quality and the nutritional value of the crops.

This patch should be planted in the sunniest spot. With limited sunlight you may opt to plant vegetables in containers or in raised beds as these can be shifted to or built within the sunny areas. A key factor to the successful cultivation of vegetables is proper soil preparation. It is therefore agreed that organic matter should be added in generous amounts to the existing soil.

Pumpkins ; A Gardening Surprise !

For the flower garden, you would have estimated the number of plants you will put in, your favourite colour scheme and the time in which the garden will be in full bloom. The same principle can be applied in the planting of the vegetables. If your garden is expected to be a mixed vegetable garden you need to concentrate the taller plants to the back of the garden. This will allow the shorter plants in the front to enjoy some filtered shade. The rows in the vegetable garden should run north to south for best sun exposure and air circulation. These gardens are equally capable of springing surprises as much as your flower gardens do. You may want to allow the surprise plant, maybe it's a pumpkin, to have its way while you patiently await the bumper crop.

Watch Your Pumpkins Grow

There is an old adage that says, "To be a successful gardener grow pumpkins." The pumpkin is a very tender vegetable. It likes a lot of water, but prefers the water to be concentrated at its roots rather than on its leaves. The pumpkin has two kinds of flowers, male and female, and the bees are their main pollinators. This lush, vigorous grower produces a main vine that can grow as long as 30 ft. and which sends out many side shoots. Wear gloves as you prune, train and redirect the vines as its leaves are slightly prickly and itchy. Prune some of the young fruits even when they are about the size of a large orange as pruning controls the energy of the plant causing it to yield fewer but larger fruits.

Pumpkins make good ground covers and at the same time they are excellent climbers. They scale the fence, climb the gate and will even venture onto the roof. Pumpkins are ready for reaping within one hundred days of planting or when the stem begins to dry or the colour of the fruit deepens. Pumpkins have a shelf life of over three months. For a fresher pumpkin leave 4-6 in. of stem on the fruit. Pumpkins are used in the production of a number of dishes such as soups, pies, breads, sauces, ice cream and beverages for immediate consumption. You may bake, roast, fry or sauté your pumpkins otherwise you may freeze or dry to preserve your harvest.

Make A Pot of Pumpkin Soup

4 cups water
1/2 lb. pumpkin (cubed or grated)
6 small dumplings
6 cubes yellow yam
1 small onion
1 cup coconut milk

1 stalk escallion
1 carrot
1 stalk thyme
2 cloves garlic
6 pimento seeds
1/2 pack Pumpkin flavoured noodle soup
1 whole scotch bonnet pepper

Soak meats overnight. Wash and cut meat, add to water in soup pot and bring to boiling point. Wash, peel and dice vegetables. Add to pot. Make dumplings, add to pot. Add milk and allow to simmer for 20 minutes. Add seasoning and simmer for another 20 minutes. Serve hot, when the aroma from the pot is unbearable . Enjoy.

THE ROSE GARDEN

"I would rather have roses on my table than Diamonds on my neck" Anonymous

A Rose bush; providing grace and charm in the landscape

Roses, christened the "Queen of Flowers" have fascinated enthusiasts for centuries. No other flower is as frequently represented, described, painted or photographed. The dramatic combination of beauty and fragrance has made it a universal obsession across all cultures and religions. Roses are vigorous shrubs with thick, thorny stems referred to as canes. The flowers are single, semi-double or double. See them in a rainbow of colours; shades of red, pink, salmon, white, yellow or orange. There is also mauve, pinkish lavender and even black; which is really a deep maroon.

Their Basic Requirements

The Rose bush requires at least 6 hours of sunlight to bloom at its best. It relishes rich, well-drained, well-aerated soil that contains an abundance of organic matter. All Rose bushes benefit from annual pruning, regular feeding and pest and disease control routine. A spot with good air circulation is ideal. Some Roses are seen as low maintenance while others are very demanding.

Planting Roses

Select the type of soil that is suitable for the variety of Rose bush chosen. Most prefer heavy yet well-drained soil. If the soil is light or contain lots of sand, marl or limestone you may amend the soil by adding compost as this will help to create moisture retentiveness to porous soils. A raised bed could be the answer to water-logged areas or you may pack a layer of small stones or broken bricks 3 ft. below the surface of the Rose bed or plant your Rose plant in large pots.

Floribunda Rose Rose

Select a suitable spot away from nearby trees that are capable of sending its roots into the soil provided for the Rose. However, trees planted in close proximity protect the rose from strong winds that can disturb and weaken the root system. Rid the area of weeds and stones. Strip off about 1 ft. of topsoil. Dig a

A showy yellow Rose

hole to a depth of 2 ft.

Prepare the soil by mixing manure with the topsoil and allowing this mix to stand for about 6 weeks to settle before planting. The roots of imported bare-root Rose bush should be soaked overnight in a solution of one gallon water and a teaspoon of sugar, or all-purpose fertilizer. This will stimulate growth. The hole should be larger than the root ball to allow the roots to spread out in their natural position. Prune damaged roots and spread the roots down and around a mound of soil in the hole. Set the plant so that the graft union is just above the soil level. Fill in the soil and eliminate air pockets. Add an inch of mulch. Water thoroughly. There must be ample space, 18-24 in. around each plant.

Propagate Them   Air Layering or Ring Barking are the most successful methods of reproducing rose plants. Grafting and Budding are also practiced. Cuttings are taken from a hardened cane that has already flowered. Use a sharp knife to cut an 8 in. long cane just below a node. Plant cuttings in equal parts of sand and peat. Keep them shaded and keep the soil moist. Manure can be used as a top dressing. Mulch with shredded bark, chopped leaves, or other organic matter to conserve moisture and to keep weeds down. Water weekly.

A Hybrid tea Rose with classic buds

A red Rose in early spring

Grandiflora rosa, obtained from a cross between hybrid teas and floribundas

Fertilizing Roses

When applying fertilizer to the newly planted bare-root Rose bush care must be taken not to burn its new roots. Apply organic amendments to the soil before and at planting time but wait until the plant has produced its first blooms to apply chemical fertilizers. Repeat after each flush of blooms. Roses relish regular applications of well rotted manure. Use a Rose fertilizer or slow release tree and shrub fertilizer and apply according to the label.

Pruning Roses

Prune the Rose bush regularly to keep them healthy and vigorous. Prune to retain as many leaves as possible and to promote a constant supply of new canes. Prune to remove dead, weak or diseased branches, as well as twiggy growth and crossed branches. Cut away canes that are over a year old and remove branches that grow inwards. Prune immediately after blooming and cut just above an outward facing bud. Pruning in spring will cut off the current season's buds. Shrub Roses are usually pruned in a vase shape.

GARDENING PASSION

Frequently Asked Questions and Answers

1. **Q. Is it possible to grow Roses in the shade?**

    A. *Some rose bush will grow in partial shade but not in dense shade. They will produce few blooms and will grow a little leggier but they will survive.*

2. **Q. How much water should I give my Roses?**

    A. *Roses love water. Water daily during spring and summer. Water in the mornings so that the plants do not spend the night being wet.*

3. **Q. How soon after planting will Roses begin to bloom?**

    A. *Six to eight weeks. Most roses bloom in late spring to early summer.*

4. **Q. Can I use Epsom salts on the Roses?**

    A. *Epsom salts promote stronger, sturdier stems, richer green foliage and deeper colours.*

5. **Q. Should I fertilize the Roses?**

    A. *Yes. Start with a liquid fertilizer at half strength. Apply fertilizer after the first blooms and once weekly, thereafter.*

6. **Q. How do I treat aphids that damage my Roses?**

    A. *Treat with insecticides, pick them off by hand or attract birds to feed on them.*

7. **Q. When should I prune my Roses?**

    A. *Prune in March or April. Wear protective gloves.*

8. **Q. My Rose is supposed to be fragrant, but it is not; what is wrong?**

    A. *Some varieties provide a fragrance but not all Roses are fragrant.*

Q-TIP PLANT

Clerodendrum quadriloculare

Blooming Q-tips

The Q-tip plant, known also as Starburst, Fireworks or Shooting Star is one of the Tropic's most beautiful flowering shrubs. It is a true "Show Stopper" as passers-by marvel at this explosion of tropical beauty. It is more often called by the common names and is part of the Verbena family of plants. This cute plant might have picked up so many names due to its blooming characteristics. This large, coarse-textured shrub originates in the Philippines. It is a fast-growing shrub that will grow into a small tree as it can reach 12-15 ft. at maturity. It is also popular amongst the butterflies, hummingbirds and bees.

For about 4-5 weeks from mid December to mid January, the Q-tip plant puts on its magnificent display that resembles an explosion of fireworks. It starts by putting out massive flower clusters of white buds on its purplish branch tips. The buds continue to elongate and reveal a bouquet of deep coral-pink tubes that open into 5 recurring light pink or white petals. The white flowers displayed against the green and purple leaves paints an extremely appealing picture. The Q-Tip plant requires regular care to stay healthy, beautiful and contained.

Planting the   Q-Tip Plant
Place this amazing eye-catcher in a location that receives full sun exposure for at least 6-8 hours per day. The plant will live in partial sun but the flowers will not be as abundant. When grown in shade the plant elongates and gets "leggy." Plant it in organically rich, well-drained and fertile soil. Water immediately after planting and then water as often as needed to keep the soil moist. This tree grows so vigorously that in most cases it will not require fertilization. You may, however, fertilize the Q-Tip plant starting in its second season. Scatter a handful of granular fertilizer around the tree and water deeply or feed with a 10-10-10 liquid fertilizer. Prune the plant in the early spring after the flowering ends as pruning encourages a full, bushy and shapely growth. Keep the soil consistently moist by mulching. This plant can be easily trained into a beautiful, small tree. The Q-Tip plant can also be grown in a container as a patio or deck plant. Your Q-Tip plant can be used as a background plant, as a fence or as a border. Uproot and pot the many suckers as gifts.

THE HIBISCUS COLLECTION

Hibiscus **blooms in a hedge**

The Hibiscus is perhaps the best known tropical shrub and flower in the world. These might have been introduced by its common names such as Roselle or Shoe Black. The varieties have green or variegated leaves which may be alternate, simple and ovate, and are often seen with a toothed or lobed margin. The colours of the trumpet-shaped flowers range from red, pink, orange, peach, purple and yellow and the hybrids are highly coloured. The 4-9 in. blooms carry single, double or elaborate blooms, often referred to as "cup and saucer". Some are also decorated with a distinguished reddish centre.

All parts of the Hibiscus flower are very influential in graphic designing and so we find these features appearing on our clothing, textile, house décors, crystals and china and in many commercials. The red hibiscus flower is traditionally worn by Tahitian women. A single bloom tucked behind the ear indicates the wearer's availability for marriage. Unaware of that meaning before writing this book, it was my habit as a married lady to wear a red hibiscus in my hair to enhance my red and white attire worn especially on Valentine's Day. Be that as it may, do enjoy your Hibiscus.

Growing Hibiscus

Although ephemeral; lasting one or two days, its showy flowers make the finest ornamental plantings for landscapes, garden beds, hedges and containers. It displays a high level of tolerance to the salty sea spray so do not be deterred if you reside on the seacoast. The Hibiscus grows flawlessly in the perfect tropical climate up to 30 ft. tall and 15 ft. wide and is known to live for more than twenty years. It adapts well to pruning and training, hence its growth in pots and suitability as Bonsai. One sure way to attract birds, butterflies and bees to your garden is to include the hibiscus; the horticultural gems.

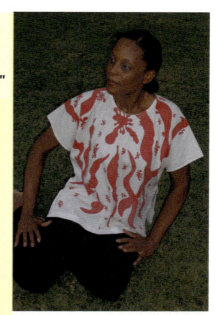

Designing

with

the

Hibiscus

Hand Crafted
Tie and Dye
"Hibiscus
"Extravaganza"

Hand Crafted Screen Printing   "Hibiscus Explosion "

The Dracaena and the Hibiscus

Hibiscus blooms in frame

Hand Crafted "Hibiscus Enshrined"

Beautiful Hibiscus Blooms In The Garden

GARDENING PASSION

Nine Questions and Answers

1. Q. How can I propagate my Hibiscus?

A. Some varieties are easily propagated while others prove to be a little stubborn. Cut the stems about 8 in. long, remove all but two small leaves. Dip the stem in rooting powder and plant. Set five to seven stems in a pot. Cover the container with a clear plastic bag. When two new leaves appear, remove bag and place the pot in the shade. When the plants are well established separate the roots under water. Air Layering and Grafting are the best methods to employ in the case of hard to propagate hybrids.

2. Q. How much sun do they need?

A. They love lots of direct sun.

3. Q. How much water do they require?

A . Hibiscus do not like wet feet, neither should you allow them to dry out.

4. Q. How much fertilizer should I apply?

A. A 10-10-10 fertilizer is good, apply weekly .

5. Q. What is the best type of soil to use?

A. A rich, sandy soil. Add manure to the soil regularly

6. Q. What cause some buds to fall before the bloom opens?

If water is lacking or in excess, if fed with too much fertilizer or if pests are attacking it.

7. Q. What are some of the pests that attack the hibiscus?

A. The thrips, aphids, whiteflies, spider mites, ants and mealy bugs. Spray with Shell White oil or with Malathion. Keep your garden clean and rid your garden of pests as soon as you notice their presence.

8 . Q. Why do leaves get yellow and fall ?

A. The leaves may be old and the plant is shedding them. Water may be sitting at the roots. Too much fertilizer was fed or insecticide was sprayed on the leaves.

9. Q. Can I grow Hibiscus in pots?

A. You can do so and with much success.

"I never had any other desire so strong and so like to covetousness, as that one which I have had always. That I might be master at last of a small house and a large garden". Anonymous

Patience is the virtue required to create an impressive landscape. Allow time for the plants to grow, for the lawns to set and for the many garden features to mellow. Allow time for the natural cohesive process to happen; for the birds to settle, the lizards and the garden spiders too.

Enjoy the growth, the exhilaration, the deserving accolades and the total satisfaction.

Landscaping is an intriguing mix of science and art. It is applied to any activity that modifies the visible features of an area of land. It includes gardening; the art of growing plants, with a goal to creating a beautiful environment. Landscaping includes working with buildings, landforms and bodies of water. Good landscape design can add to the value of the house, dramatically increases the living space and contributes greatly to improved lifestyles. It is a functional outdoor art and a living, breathing entity.

Designing the Landscape

Landscape designing is hardly mystical. You need to observe the contours of your property, note how the natural light falls throughout the day and the influential presence of permanent structures such as porches, driveways and walkways. Set the basic parameters of your house and yard and interchange different landscaping features. See how trees, shrubs and plants will affect these features when all entities come into play. The front yard and the backyard usually constitute separate functions. The front yard is about creating a stunning facade; to enhance your house and to increase its value. The backyard is to increase the livable space; for relaxation, for privacy and for practical enjoyment. Be creative and incorporate elements from different traditional styles.

1. Formal Garden : The Formal Garden style follows symmetrical patterns with lines, precise geometric shapes, obvious colour choice, order, well-groomed plants, lawns and hedges. You will often find topiary and bonsai art forms, water features and gazebos in these landscapes. This landscaping style requires a lot of maintenance.. **2. English Garden :** The English Garden style uses shrubs and perennials to complement the architectural style of the house. Arbours are also included. **3. Oriental Garden:** The Oriental Garden style uses water, rocks and evergreen plants. It often includes the Japanese Zen garden. **4. Informal Garden:** The Informal garden style uses assorted garden beds with curved lines. Plants, furniture and garden ornaments are seemingly randomly arranged lines.

5. **Woodland Garden:** Woodland Garden style has a less manicured appearance; as the flora and fauna are kept as natural and undisturbed.

Maintaining the Landscape

There is no landscape that is maintenance free. There are two kinds of landscapes; those with gardens that make you feel at peace and those that are jarring and chaotic.

Buildings : Keep buildings freshly painted and the ponds and pools clean.

Planting areas : Keep hedges, borders and partitions groomed.

Insects : Spray with natural insecticide to control insects and pests.

Weeds : Weeds are a nuisance; eliminate them by digging out the entire root.

The Lawn : Mow the lawn regularly to maintain the look. Some mowers are designed with a bag that collects the grass and unwanted seeds.

Leaves : Pick up the leaves. The layer of leaves can restrict the amount of light reaching the lawn and trap water near the roots. It can also be unsightly.

Extraordinary silhouettes in the landscape

Naturally formed Floral Designs In the Land-scape

Position the sun-loving Vanda Orchid in the sun

Oncidium Orchid in semi-shade

Boughtonia orchid
(indigenous to Jamaica)

GARDENING PASSION

Place

the

Phalaenopis

(Moth

Orchid)

in

dappled

light

Staghorn fern mounted on a tree

Place those plants with delicate blooms in dappled shade

Desert Rose grown in container and placed in full sun

Dendrobium orchid mounted on a tree

Vanilla fragrans (planifolia) (Orchid) It produces a long, slender, pod-like fruit from which the Vanilla spice is derived

Dendrobium Orchid (Blue) vies for optimal attention

ELEMENTS and PRINICIPLES of LANDSCAPE DESIGN

Landscaping like all other works of art, rests on elements that serve as the building blocks of design and principles that should be observed to create an aesthetically pleasing product. Elements are the basic visual materials such as colour, lines, form, texture and scale used to establish a design. **Elements** are the basic visual materials used to establish a design. The five elements are **colour, lines, form, texture and scale.**

Colour is used to convey emotion and to influence moods. It is the most striking aspect of any landscape design. Bright colours like red, yellow and orange seem to jump out at you and direct your attention to a specific spot, while cool colours like green and blue seem to make the object recede. A landscape can look harsh if the colours are not properly chosen, if the choice of colour is too varied and if the colours are inappropriately placed.

Yellow Poui (Tabebuia serratifolia)

Colours should not be spotted around as a patchy, confused appearance will result. Instead it should be concentrated with its shades and tones in one area with opportunities created for them to merge into the another colour. Colours for the garden should also be selected to enhance the colour of the house. Being aware of the time of blooming and the duration of the blooms will allow you to choose between annuals that will produce instant gratification or perennials that will be long-term investments. You may opt to select a mix of both, which will guarantee a spurt of colours all year round.

Lines create order by propelling the eyes to a focal point. Lines define and separate garden beds, paths and driveways. Whether straight or curved, lines become essential in the structural design of the landscape. Straight lines are forceful and direct, while curved lines are more natural, gentle and have a moving and flowing effect. Lines are used to direct attention to objects, divide a space, group like- objects or separate unrelated objects.

Forms may be round, spreading, pyramidal, oval, columnar or even drooping. The choice of trees, shrubs, flowers and garden accessories will create that sense of form. Natural forms will change their shapes and characteristics and will require training and pruning to maintain the desired look.

Scale is the size of an object in relationship to its surroundings. As a general rule in landscape design, plants and structures should be proportional to the human scale.

Textures relate to the coarseness or fineness, the ruggedness or smoothness, the sheen or dulness of an item. Tree trunks, leaves, flowers, stems, stones, are all uniquely textured. Textured items that contrast or complement are the basis of a good design.

An aged tree with clinging plants, dangling vines and varied textures

GARDENING PASSION

Principles make use of the elements to create functionality and appeal. The seven principles of a well designed landscape are embedded in **unity, balance, proportion, focalization or emphasis, sequence or transition, rhythm and repetition**. One is not required to apply every principle. It is however, beneficial to have an understanding of these principles, as this will help to generate ideas and increase creativity.

Applying the Principles

Unity should be your main goal when applying the principles of design. This is achieved by maintaining the consistency of the character of chosen elements in the design. Create unity by developing a garden theme. Should you embrace a water theme, then you may highlight the theme by installing a range of water features. Repeat the same plant or plant group, the same garden décor or the same colour for continuity. Unity is achieved when all the different elements fit together to make a complete or unified picture.

Balance is an even distribution or an equal amount. Balance can be symmetrical (formal) or it can be asymmetrical (informal). In a **symmetrical design** the left side arrangement will be identical to the right side arrangement. Let's go back to the art class at school and recall those instances when you took a piece of paper, splashed paint on it, folded it in two equal parts, opened it and found an interesting symmetrical design. We may therefore describe symmetrical as a mirror image. On the other hand, **asymmetrical design** would not be identical on each side and may be described as unbalanced. One can create unity and balance by having the same number of points of interest. It is possible to balance the landscape with shade trees on one side and low growing gardens on the other side.

Norfolk Island Pine; perfectly symmetrical

The linking factors that will create the unity will be the rocks, plants, ground covers and décor. Plant height, colour, form and texture may vary at each side but should be consistent.

Proportion is keeping the landscape features in scale with the house and the land space. Keep in mind the ultimate size of trees and shrubs as they spread and tower over time. Ornaments should be carefully selected as enormous garden statures will be out of proportion when placed in a small front yard. On the other hand a small feature will fit proportionately in a large area, when it creates its own distinct space. Proportion helps to strike balance and harmony, while creating a pleasing relationship among the three dimensions, that of length, breadth and height. Smart usage of space will allow a garden to look balanced and proportionate.

Focalization directs visual attention to a point of interest. This focal point may be achieved by using contrasting colours or by the placement of an item of interest.

Sequence or transition creates visual movement. This can be achieved by the gradual progression of texture, form, size or colour. Transition may also be used to create depth or distance.

Rhythm creates a feeling of motion. This motion leads the eye from one part of the landscape to another. Rhythm may be achieved by the repetition of colours, shape, texture, line or form.

Repetition is the repeated use of objects or elements with identical shape, form, texture or colour. Repetition can lead to rhythm, focalization or emphasis, but can also be overdone.

A river meanders through and creates a point of interest

GARDENING BLUNDERS

With much anxiety to establish a garden, one tends to quickly grasp the opportunity to do so without applying the requirements; that of planning and preparation. Having used that hasty approach, one finds later that a number of things could have been done differently. Blunders, poor choices and mistakes can ruin the gardening pleasures. Some of these mistakes may be corrected without much hassle, while the correction of others may be time consuming, difficult and expensive.

- **Not drawing a plan:** Failure to plan can result in a 'helter-skelter,' confusing, unattractive and awkward garden design. The placement of buildings, designated areas, trees, garden beds, garden features and décor, aught to be mapped out on paper in advance.

- **Insufficient attention to soil fertility:** One should loosen or till the soil to a depth of 12 in. and incorporate several inches of compost before planting.

- **Not mulching:** The use of mulch is sometimes ignored much to the detriment of the plants. Use organic mulch which makes your plants less stressed. As the mulch breaks down it adds more nutrients and improve the soil quality.

- **Too much fertilizer:** Over enthusiasm to see your plants grow can motivate you to use too much fertilizer. This can cause the plants to be more susceptible to pests and diseases.

- **Wrong selection of plants:** Consider the plants as they relate to the soil type, the terrain, the general climatic condition and the colour scheme. Take note of the amount of sun or shade the premises offer, the amount of time that the plants will require your care and the fragrance you seek.

- **Purchasing contaminated or infected plants:** Ensure that the new plants you bring to your garden are free of pests and diseases, as these will spread to your healthy plants.

- **Not providing adequate space:** Planting a tree without considering its size at maturity will result in inadequate space for the plant. The ultimate size of the tree is of utmost importance.

- **Pruning at the wrong time :** Prune in spring after the blooming season is over.

- **Planting in pots without drainage holes :** Open holes in pots to allow excess water to run out.
- **Weeding errors :** Sometimes it is hard to distinguish your plant. Make markers using icicle sticks marked with a permanent marker or pen.
- **Not giving plants enough sun:** Some plants need at least 6 hours of direct sun, otherwise they will not bloom.
- **Wrong plant location:** The matter of sticking a plant; especially a permanent tree, here and there, will not necessarily create the design principles that make for a well-designed garden. Later it may be deemed as totally out of place.
- **Neglecting new plant:** A plant can only thrive on the care it receives. Remember to plant in the best soil, water as required, feed appropriately and place in the best location.
- **Lack of plant knowledge:** Insufficient knowledge will result in lack of care which can cause the demise of the plant. Conduct research and learn about your plants.
- **Under or Over Watering :** Different plants require different amounts of water. Inadequate water will dehydrate the plants while excess water will drown the roots or cause root rot. Learn about their water requirements and supply appropriately.
- **Untimely potting:** When the roots have out grown the pot, you should repot in a slightly larger pot. Ignoring this can lead to a root bound plant.
- **Ignoring wildlife:** The presence of birds, bees and butterflies create movement, frolic and sound so encourage them. Provide them with water and food.
- **Improper combination of plant species:** Have a good combination of perennials to keep your garden alive with flowers. Perennials are seasonal bloomers. Annuals are "quick fixes," so within three months most annuals will set the gardens ablaze.
- **Poor record keeping:** Failure to keep planting and blooming records can cause unnecessary expenditure, as the home garden can supply the flowers needed for special occasions.

Plants placed too close to the driveway

- **Planting close to the driveway:** This may even hinder you from opening the car door fully and exiting the car without damaging the plants.

- **Excluding fruit trees :** Fruit trees supply loads of fruits. Designate an area to be cultivated as an orchard. Train, prune and keep each tree low so that fruits are within arms reach. Some fruit trees are very ornamental, the blooms fall to the ground and form a thick colourful layer.

- **Excluding shade trees :** Shade trees make a garden comfortable for the people, the plants and the wild life. Select strategic locations to plant them.

- **Inadequate plumbing and irrigation systems:** My secret to a crisp, green, healthy looking garden, is to keep it properly watered. The watering process should then be made as easy as possible, by installing water within easy reach. An automatic irrigation system is extremely convenient. This system can also be used to serve the water features you add to the garden.

- **Not constructing retaining walls before planting :** If you are unsure about the stability of a slope do not risk the possible loss of a building or some valuable plants. Rain is unpredictable and sometimes will fall for several days, increasing the risk of a land slippage. A wall will save the loss of soil and prevent deformity of the landscape.

- **Not maximizing available resources:** You may be forced to contend with land space that has an influx of boulders is too shaded by massive trees or is in the full grasp of the scorching sun. It may have the characteristics of a tame forest, is set on a slope or has a stream running through. See these features as powerful assets. It is time to bridge the waters and to create a covetous garden.

- **Installing garden features because others have done so:** Installing expensive garden features could prove to be a foolish idea as these are not obligatory features in landscaping designs. The aim is to make the landscape a simple and beautiful picture that will enhance your home.

- **Not enclosing the property:** Strayed and wild animals are culprits that often come in and with a grudge, they unscrupulously deform the landscape. It is therefore imperative that proper fencing and gates are installed thus saving you getting out of bed at odd hours of the night to chase them away.

Strayed animal

- **Inappropriate tools:** Gardening is an ongoing adventure, so some specific tools will always be needed. They make gardening easier and safer. It is important that all the necessary tools and protective gears are procured, organized and stacked away until needed.

- **Failing to remember the other functions of the landscape:** A well designed garden not only serves to satisfy aesthetically, but will encourage individuals to find reasons to encourage social interaction at such a beautiful place. Functionality is one good

Not procuring gloves required for this job

- feature, so the well- designed garden should now be ready to play dual roles, that of functionality and aesthetics.

- **Not removing the clutter:** Rubble is not only unsightly, but will also result in the infestation of rodents and insects. With the garbage removed there will be no need to use insecticides.

- **Not maintaining the lawns and the garden beds:** A well-groomed lawn is the backbone of the landscape and should not be neglected ? Why allow the weeds to capture the garden and choke the plants? It is easier and less time consuming to cut the lawn and groom all plants on a regular basis, than to clear an overgrowth of what turns out to be a forest in the making.

- **Planting invasive plants:** Some plants if allowed, will overrun the garden. These plants are best grown in containers.

ESSENTIAL GARDENING TOOLS

After deciding that digging with their bare hands was a slow and painful nightmare, our ingenious forefathers invented their own tools made of wood, flint and bone. Today we are bewildered by the array of available and durable tools made of metal, copper, iron and steel. The kind of gardening equipment required will depend on the size and extent of the gardening project. Tools should be selected to complement the kind of work to be accomplished. Modern gardening tools help to keep your garden in a good state. Tools help to prepare good growing conditions required for the plant's health. There are tools for different jobs in the garden.

Hand tools, power tools, cutting tools, pruning tools, carrying tools and watering tools are some general categories. The spade, garden hoe, garden fork, rake and a plough are necessary, so are the hedge trimmers, sweepers, lawn aerators, irrigation sprinklers, mini tractors and the lawn mowers. The wheelbarrow will help to transport both your tools and plant cuttings to and from the garden. Despite their importance, garden tools are probably the most neglected tools because after their use they are often put away quite dirty and wet. However, with proper maintenance our tools can last for many generations. Among other gardening niceties are the watering can, boots, slippers, aprons, goggles, caps and gloves. Gloves will help to save your hands from any unforeseen accident and the gardening knee pad will save your knees from injury.

(1) Shear (2) Secateurs (3) Hand Trowel

(4) Hand Fork (5) Hand Shovel

Tips To Prolong The Use Of Gardening Tools

- Avoid leaving the tools outside; store in tool shed.
- Cleaned tools last longer so wash the tools after every use to remove soil and chemical residue. Chemicals and fertilizers will cause corrosion to metal.
- Dry tools in the sun or with a towel, as water will rust metal and rot wooden handles.
- Rub linseed oil on the wooden parts to prevent drying out or splitting and wipe metal parts of hand tools with an oily rag.
- Store large digging tools in a bucket filled with dry builder's sand and a little oil to lubricate.
- Use a large garbage can or barrel to store rakes, brooms or other long-handled tools
- Keep tools sharpened. A machete file or a sharpening stone will produce good results.
- Remove rust with a steel brush, sand paper or steel wool. Wear protective gloves and goggles.
- Use sand paper to rub the splints away from damaged or splintered wooden handles.
- Hang tools that are made for hanging.
- Periodically tighten screws on shears, pruners, weed whackers and lawn mowers.
- Never leave the garden hose outside during the hot sun or the cold season, as this increases the chances of it springing leaks.
- Find tools easier by giving the handles a coat of bright colours.
- Avoid leaving tools on the floor of garages or in damp places.
- Use plastic containers, such as the dish drainers to hold small tools.
- Drain all gas-powered tools of oil and fuel before seasonal or long-term storage.
- Do not allow chemicals to remain on the tools.

Lawn Mower

GARDENING PASSION

THE BEST SOIL

Regard your soil as a living entity, as it too needs food and water. It contains the three main nutrients: Nitrogen, Phosphorus and Potassium which are vital to growing plants. It is incumbent on us to protect the soil structure, feed the soil with nutrients from natural sources and increase the number of organisms that live in the soil. Rich, medium and well-drained soil gives best results. Best fruits and blooms are produced in soil containing 5 -10 % lime and sufficient quantities of iron. The fertility of the soil is dependent on its physical and chemical characteristics. Hence, soil that is poor and has a hard substratum should be avoided or sufficiently amended before it is used. **Loam soil** is a mix of sand, silt or clay and organic matter. It is loose and looks rich. When squeezed in the fist, moist loam will form a ball which crumbles when poked with a finger. Loam soil absorbs water and stores moisture well. **Clay and silt soils** are made of very small particles. They feel sticky when wet. Clay and silt hold moisture well but resist water infiltration when dry. **Sandy soils** contain large, sandy particles which are visible to the naked eye and are usually light in colour. Sandy soils stay loose and allow moisture to penetrate easily but do not retain it for long.

Soil Drainage Test Plants that are suitable for the home landscape do not like" wet feet."

Unsuitable soil should be drained, amended or avoided. Test to ascertain the drainage quality.

1. Dig a hole in the planting area, fill it with water and watch the water drain away.

2. If the water does not soak away in 2 hours, there is a drainage problem.

3. Drainage is excellent when the water drains away within 20-60 minutes.

4. Drainage is regarded as adequate when the water is not there after 6 hours.

5. If after 24 hours the water is still sitting there, then there is a major drainage problem.

Amendments are added to the soil to improve the nutrient levels, the drainage capabilities and the pH. Soil pH is a basic property that affects many chemicals and biological activities in the soil. The degree of acidity or alkalinity is known as the soil pH. A soil with a pH of 7.0 is regarded as neutral. Most plants grow best with a neutral pH of between 6 and 8. If the pH is off in either direction, plants will not grow, fruit or bloom as they should. The scale used to determine the contents runs from 0, which is highly acidic, to 14.0, which is pure alkaline. Spring is the best season to mix amendments into the soil. Consider these factors when selecting a soil for amendment:

1. The duration: the length of time the amendment will last in the soil. **2.** The soil texture.

3. The soil salinity and plant sensitivity to salts. **4.** The salt content. **5.** The pH of the amendment.

Amending the Soil
There are two broad categories of soil amendments; the organic and the inorganic. Organic amendments are developed from something that is or was alive, such as sphagnum peat, wood chips, straw, compost, manure and sawdust. These amendments increase the soil organic content and offer many benefits such as soil aeration, water infiltration and both water and nutrient holding capacity. These amendments contain plant nutrients, act as organic fertilizer and are also energy sources for bacteria, fungi and earthworms which are beneficial to the soil. Livestock manures are valuable additions to soil as their nutrients are immediately available to soil organisms and plants. Inorganic amendments are either mined or man-made and include perlite, shells, 1/2in. size gravel and sand.

Soil types that need amendment
Soil that drains well: Add organic matter every 3-4 years to maintain its good consistency and boost nutrient levels. Apply a 2-3 in. deep layer of organic matter. **2.** *Fast-draining soil:* Add organic matter to improve nutrient levels and slow the drainage rate. Use sphagnum peat, well-aged manure or compost. **3.** *Soil that has poor drainage capabilities:* Add organic matter and some perlite or sand every year. Add a 3 in. layer of organic matter to improve drainage.

4. Soil with too much sulphur or lime: After the soil has been tested for it pH, salt and nutrients add organic matter to make it more acidic or alkaline or to improve its nutrient levels.

Some Common Amendments
Lime (white lime) is limestone that has been melted or ground up to make it easier to integrate in the soil. It is used to change the pH of the soil, either to make an acidic soil neutral for general plant growth or to make a neutral soil alkaline.

Sawdust and wood shaving are cuttings from mature trees. They will take about a year to decompose This is sufficient time for it to mellow.

Wood ash is ashes obtained from burning wood. It contains potash and phosphate. It is capable of burning seedlings and roots. Use this sparingly as excessive use can cause toxicity problems. It is an alkaline material, so wear a pair of gloves, a dust mask and an eye protector when applying it. Do not mix it with man-made fertilizer. Avoid spreading wood ash on a windy day.

Coarse sand or builder's sand are obtained from rivers or beaches. It can be added to clay to improve the soil texture. Improvement will be noticeable over a period of time. Till the soil and add a generous amount of coarse sand and some organic matter.

Animal waste are the droppings of the horse, sheep, poultry, rabbit, guinea pig and rat-bat. These droppings are very toxic and must be made to sit for at least three-months before it is used. It should not be applied directly to the growing plants, but should be tilled into the soil. This manure is a source of bad weeds and unwanted seeds and is best processed in a hot pile or in a big garbage bag that is placed in the sun for a few months. Animal waste constitutes an excellent soil amendment.

Compost is the decomposition of plant remains and animal waste into vital nutrients. It is used primarily as a soil conditioner. Compost loosens the soil, making it more pliable and manageable. Keep mulch approximately 4 in. away from the stem or trunks of plants. A well-mulched garden can yield 50% more than one that is not.

Composting Tips

1. Keep the compost bin covered. **2.** Air is important in the process so allow air to pass through the bin. Do this by cutting holes in the containers and giving the heap a monthly mix. **3.** Compost is warm, even hot, don't be alarmed at the heat that will emit when you stir the heap. **4.** Put a few bricks or stones at the base of the container to encourage drainage. **5.** Avoid limbs, sticks or any tough material that will take too long to break down. **6.** Compost must be kept damp but not wet. Wet compost may give off an odour, so cover the bin with crumbled or shredded newspaper. Place the covered bin in a corner. **7.** Keep compost away from direct sunlight. **8.** Beetles, bacteria, fungi and earthworms are all workers in the breaking down process and should be left to complete their duties. **9.** Centipedes sometimes live in the compost. they will sting, avoid them.

The compost is ready when it is dark, rich looking, broken down, crumbles and smells like earth. The process can take from 6 weeks to a year. The more air circulation and bacteria the compost pile receives, the faster the material is able to break down. When the compost pit is dry, water can be added to the pit to hasten decomposition in the lower section. The long process can be decreased by the addition of chemical activators that are available on the market.

Make A Compost Heap

Compost is prepared or stored in large plastic containers, wooden barrels or large plastic bags. A shallow hole dug in the ground provides for an open heap that can be covered with a plastic lid. Compost bins can be purchased at garden centres or at hardware stores. The best ingredients for the compost heap are grass cuttings, weeds without seeds, dried leaves, food, fruits and vegetable peelings. Add also, a handful of charcoal and some shredded newspaper. Droppings from herbivorous animals will serve as the sugar and spice needed to complete this recipe. Do not use cooked foods, meats, fish, soot or magazine pages, nor the droppings of dogs and cats. Some leaves, such as the mango leaves are tough and do not break down before 2 years so it is best to eliminate these.

Mulch The Organic Way

Almond leaves

Coconut shells

Dried grass

Sea almond husks

Wood shavings

Horse manure

Mulch is a layer of material spread evenly on the surface soil. The use of mulch has been a long established horticultural practice. Mulch can be classified as organic and inorganic. Organic mulch is comprised of organic materials; which can be broken down while inorganic consist of materials that will not break down. With time, organic mulch decomposes and enriches the soil. Turn the mulch over as soon as the gardening season is over, so it breaks down before the garden is replanted.

Mulching improves the soil quality and supplies minerals and other elements which are essential for plant growth. This however, should not take the place of fertilizer as organic mulch is deficient of some nutrients. Mulch can be applied anytime. Two inches is the recommended depth for mulching. At this depth most mulch will achieve the primary objectives of weed control and soil moisture conservation. Mulch that is laid too thick will reduce the drying out time especially during the rainy season.

The objectives of mulching are to:

1. Block out sunlight to weeds and seedlings thus reducing their growth.

2. Keep soil cool and moist. 3. Provide material that will eventually break down to form organic matter on the top layer.

4. Help to prevent the soil from getting compact. 5. Protect young plants from diseases. 6. Keep slugs from attacking plants. 7. Increase the aesthetics of the landscape. 8. Add to the property value. 9. Give the garden a clean and tidy appearance.

Hard to control weeds may come through the mulched layer but can be pulled through more easily. Adding organic material makes the soil more crumbly, especially clay soils that are hard and compact. A patch of vegetables will harvest more since there would be less food rot as fruits or vegetables would not touch the soil, neither would soil be splashed on to the fruits. These fruits would also be easier to harvest and less likely to be bruised during harvesting.

ESTABLISHING THE LAWN

Very often, the lawn which is designed for aesthetic and recreational purposes constitutes the biggest feature of the landscape. The lawn is really grass that is used as a ground cover. The grass is usually carefully selected and planted under the best conditions, then watered, fed and mowed regularly, resulting in a beautiful, lush and green lawn. The preparation that is put in at the initial stage will determine the quality and appearance of the end product and the amount of maintenance that will be required. Design the lawn using straight or gradually curved lines, as this is easier to maintain. Avoid sudden or sharp turns.

Lush, green lawn humidified by a river and shaded by overhanging trees

It is time to prepare the surface. The hunt is now on for the best surface soil, known in horticultural and agricultural parlance as topsoil. This soil is better textured and loaded with minerals and nutrients. It is best to have the soil tested. If found to be too high in acid, I lb. white lime may be added to each 20 sq. ft. of soil. If the soil quality is poor some fertilizer; chemical or organic fertilizer should be worked into 8-12 in. of the soil. When adding topsoil, ensure that it is mixed deep into the soil and not just laid on the top. When establishing a big lawn it may be necessary to employ the use of a tiller otherwise, a garden fork will do. A stone or steel rake will be very handy in filling out the low areas, breaking down bumps and removing lumps, foreign bodies and stones. A subtle grade should be created to channel water runoff. For big lawns, an underground gravel path can be installed as drainage for excess water. This is the best time to install the plumbing system.

Select The Grass
Grasses are available in a variety of species. Some grass species are tough and durable, some lush and green, some prefer the full sun, while others are quite comfortable in light shade. The Zoysia and the Bermuda species are often used. **Zoysia** is a creeping, slow growing, warm season grass that, with proper maintenance, will produce a rich, green colour. It is very invasive and will crowd out all other species in the lawn. It forms a dense grass that limits weed encroachment. It performs well in full sun and partial shade. Zoysia prefers moderately loose soils for peak performance. Though drought tolerant, it requires weekly watering. In sandy soils it requires more frequent watering. Water during the morning as watering at night is likely to cause fungal development. **Bermuda grass,** (Cynodon dactylon) is a popular ground cover with short, flat leaves. It is used for lawns, golf courses, sporting fields and parks. This grass is resistant to drought and if watered will maintain its colour through periods of drought. During the hot months the grass aught to be watered twice weekly to maintain its colour. If allowed Bermuda grass usually grows 4-16 in. tall. It creeps along the ground, rooting wherever it touches the soil, forming a dense mat. It has a strong root system that can grow more than 4 ft. deep. It is very durable in high traffic areas.

Carpet or Crabgrass (Axonopus compressus) is unpopular with many gardeners, because it can be very invasive. The roots can also travel several feet under plastic sheeting or paved driveways until they find an opening to get above ground.

Planting Grass
Lawns may be established by seeding, transplanting or planting seedlings. The best time to sow grass seeds is during April to May and September to October, as there is ample rainfall during these months. Grass seeds differ in size so the amount used per square will differ. Scatter the seeds and use a fan rake to lightly rake the seeds into the surface of the soil. If the seeds are very fine and may not spread as sparsely as you would have them, then you may mix the seeds with some dry sand and scatter evenly. The best way to spread the seeds evenly is to do it twice. To do this effectively you should spread the seeds first in one direction and the second time in the opposite direction. The seeds will germinate within 5-28 days of planting.

Cover With Turfs: Instead of planting seeds and waiting for twenty days for them to germinate, one may opt to take the short cut method of procuring turfs of grass and laying these down. This will complete the lawn in a single day. Water daily, until rooted.

Plant Sprigs : The planting of sprigs is practiced on small lawns. Plant sprigs 6-8 in. apart, so that they will have space to spread and eventually fill the whole area. Firm the soil around the roots and add some clean, weed-free mulch.

Water the Lawn: Whatever method you use, you will need to water immediately after planting. Most lawns need about 2 in. water weekly in a hot climate. Too much water will harm the grass seeds; use just enough water to allow them to grow.

Fertilize the Lawn: Most lawn grasses grow vigorously and may need additional amounts of nutrients in order to stay looking nice. Fertilize after the seeds have established their roots. When the lawn is well established, mow the lawn.

CHAPTER SIX

GARDENING AESTHETICS

"More than anything I must have flowers always"
Claude Monet

Aesthetics is the primary factor most landscapers consider when planning a garden. The art, beauty and flair should make your creation appear as natural as possible. Apart from the visual aesthetics, a wide variety of other sensory experiences can be enhanced by the careful selection of plants based on the colour of their foliage and blooms. Aesthetics is very important in ensuring beauty and tranquility in the garden. Gardening aesthetics is another form of creating and playing with the elements and principles of design. The gardens surrounding your home are expressions of your sense of aesthetics, your values and your vision of comfort. It is your personal message to the community. It tells everything about you. It is instinctive to create places where we want to spend time, both in and outside of the home. If we feel overwhelmed by a confusing, unkempt garden we may spend less time there. If we are made to feel good in a beautiful landscape, even if we are new to learning its many functions, then we will spend more quality time there.

Colour, is the most prominent factor in the garden aesthetics and is often the first thing considered. It is an integral part of the decorating process. Our reaction and feeling toward colour is universal. Colour in the landscape provided by flowers, foliage or architecture will invoke a deep sense of satisfaction. Use softer and earthy colours to create a soothing, personal space or in contrast, use bolder colours for an exciting and entertaining space. A simple dash of colour on dull pieces of furnishing or on a pot can tie scattered elements to the landscape, can attract birds, bees and butterflies and can create wonderful moods.

Orchid blooms creating drifts of colours

A BUBBLY LOOK AT COLOURS

- **Primary colours** include red, yellow and blue. These bright colours energize the garden and will attract the eye from a great distance. Red is deemed so wonderful colour, it is also a difficult colour to use on a large scale. It denotes love, friendship and prosperity.

- **Warm colours** include red, orange and yellow. They tend to make flowers appear closer than they really are. Yellows are joyful and warm and harmonize very well with greens.

- **Cool colours** such as blue, violet and silver lend a cool, calming effect and make plants appear farther away; for that effect use blue and white together.

- **A monochromatic colour scheme** is composed of plants of the same colour. This is best done by using a mix of tones or shades of the same colour in addition to various textures, shapes and sizes.

- **Complementary colours** are opposite from each other on the colour wheel. These are high in contrast and add drama and excitement. Combinations of yellow and violet, orange and blue or green and red varieties are examples of complementary colours.

- **Harmonious colours** have a soothing effect. These combinations include blue and violet, orange and red and orange and yellow. These colours unify a garden.

- **Foliage colours** of green dominate the garden and are refreshing when used alone. Green is dramatic with red and harmonizes well with yellow and blue. Bronze, silver, reddish-purple foliage add a bold element to your garden.

- **White** is classy. It blends well with every colour and can be used as a transition between colours that do not normally work well together. It is very noticeable in a border or fence.

- **Pastels** and **muted colours** set a tranquil mood in soft pink, lavender, lilac and peach.

An Astounding Array of Colours in the Garden

GARDENING PASSION

Colourful Foliage in the Garden

GARDENING PASSION

White Blooms in the Garden

Splash Colours With Bright Blooms

Annuals produce more blooms than the other types of flowering plants. They flower earlier in their life cycle and they also produce blooms that last for over several weeks. They are among the most beautiful and colourful of all flowers and they are very popular with both the new and the experienced gardeners.

Marigold to brighten the garden

Find them a place in the sun and every one of these plants will delight you with beautiful colours week after week. Get away from the usual calmness of white, blues and purples, put in some intense colours and fill the garden beds with flame-coloured annuals. To propagate themselves from season to season, these easy to grow annuals produce great quantities of seeds. If the flowers are cut before seeds are formed, another set of blooms will rapidly grow to assure a seed crop. Sowing of seeds in early months will ensure that some annuals are in bloom throughout the year.

Annuals and biennials fill in with quick growth and colourful flowers, while perennials and foundation plantings take time to grow to their mature size. They are ideal for filling bare spaces between trees, to furnish gorgeous hues and to augment the shorter bloom-time of most perennials. Plant them wherever people gather around the seating areas, near the gazebo and make it easy to embrace the lavish burst of colours and delicate fragrance. The variety of foliage colour and texture will provide a contrast and will keep the garden exciting through out the year. Dahlias, Zinnias, Cosmos, Marigolds and Sunflowers will produce swirls of exciting colours. Use annuals to supply instant flowers and for temporary camouflage around the less attractive places.

Some perennials produce delicate flowers while others produce robust bright-coloured bunches. Perennials form the backbone to any landscape. Unlike annuals, perennials last for more than 2 years. They are referred to as herbaceous perennials, because they lack woody stems. Trees and shrubs are referred to as woody perennials because they do have woody stems and trunks. Hardy herbaceous perennials will provide instant colour to invigorate the garden. They are ideal for the container or for planting in borders, hedges or in garden beds. Bulbs are also categorized as perennials, some of which include Lilies and Iris. Use perennials to create a colour-filled backdrop, noting that the tallest plants when placed in the back offer height, dignity and interest.

TRAINING AND PRUNING PLANTS

Pruning is the removal of a portion of a plant so as to maintain its structure. It involves the removal of parts that are not required, are ineffective or of no use to the plant. It encompasses a number of horticultural techniques that are used on fruit-bearing, ornamental trees and on flowering plants. It is a fairly new practice in which plant growth is directed into a desired shape, height and form. This practice will improve the general form and character of the plant while enhancing the landscape and upgrading its value. Pruning and training ornamentals, fruit trees and shrubs are essential to proper tree development, strong branch structure, reduction of disease infestation, increased ventilation and the stimulation of new growth for an abundant harvest.

This procedure should begin the first year after transplanting and should take place gradually over several years. Older, neglected trees are more difficult, dangerous and expensive to prune and should be done when plants are in the dormant stage. Over-pruned trees will produce light crops of large, flavourless fruits that do not store well. Pruning should be carried out to achieve a balance between shoot growth and fruit production. Be reminded that thinning is better than shearing, so cut back to a bud, a lateral branch or to the main trunk. Avoid leaving a stub.

Pruning

Pruning is done to achieve uniformity by removing :

- Overlapping branches and twiggy growth.

- Branches that grow downwards.

- Branches that have been damaged by insects, disease or wind.

- Branches that shoot from the base or trunk.

- Any upright shoots that may appear at the root of the tree.

- Weak branches and dry limbs.

Prune deeply to achieve desired size, and allow new growth

The Benefits of Pruning

1. Yields high quality fruits, early blooms, good plant health and long plant life.
2. Develops a strong tree framework that will support fruit and bloom production.
3. Removes dead, diseased or broken limbs.
4. Opens up the tree canopy to maximize light penetration, essential for overall development.
5. Permits adequate air movement through the tree to which promotes rapid drying.
6. Clears obstruction to views and prevents overcrowding.
7. Provides aesthetically pleasing plants.
8. Provides geometrically and artistically shaped plants in the garden.

Sterilize all pruning tools after each cut to prevent the spreading of disease. The ideal sterilization solution is made up of 1 part bleach to 9 parts water.

Topiary

The whimsical art form known as Topiary, is the horticultural discipline of training live perennial plants to develop and maintain clearly defined shapes. It is the skillful twisting of twigs of trees and shrubs into geometric or fanciful forms. Topiary encompasses small portable plantings which add interesting accents to the landscape This gardening art form is a type of living sculpture. Traditional shapes include cubes, pyramids and cones. However it is the talented topiary artist, who, with an eye for symmetry, designs spirals, boxes, people and animals

An 'on the ladder view' of a manicured Topiary fence

by weaving together the stems of two or three plants, followed by regular clipping or training into desired shapes. There are two kinds of topiary: vine and shrub.

Topiary Made With Vines

1. Choose a topiary form.

2. Choose a plant such as the English Ivy or the Boston Ivy. The English Ivy grows quickly, is tolerant of many conditions and looks lovely.

3 Fill the form with sphagnum moss, fine wood shaving or dried grass.

4. Plant the vine around the form and allow it to crawl up the form and cover the shape.

5. Train the vines to wrap around the form.

6. Pinch back any unruly shoot.

Topiary Made With Shrubs

Choose the plant. The Ficus, Boxwood, Creeping fig, Lavender, Myrtle, Pine, Rosemary and Yew are most suitable for this art form. These make fine topiary designs because they have small leaves, tight growth patterns and are evergreen. You may start with a small shrub, but a grown plant will do. You may buy frames in a garden store or fashion one from old toys, metal frames, broken garden statues or bamboo. Frames are often constructed with plastic or coated steel wire. Clothes hangers make suitable frames for those starting a project at home or at school. Topiary is an interesting art form for children

A topiary green fence designed as a backdrop

and they will enjoy making the frames. The frame you select or make depends largely on the type of topiary you desire. Put the topiary form over the shrub you choose to sculpt. The frame will help to guide you as you prune. You may create topiary without a topiary form but a frame makes it easier.

Training the Topiary

Pruning will encourage additional and bushier growth. On a small shrub, prune 1 in. off in areas where you need to fill in. On shaping a large shrub, take no more than 3 in. off areas where you wish to cut back. Deeper cuts may ruin the process. Train and prune the shrub every 3 months during active growth. Adequate irrigation and ample sunlight will generate the desired outcome. Add interest to the topiary by under planting with other plants. Integrate such projects in art classes and in the 4-H Club programme. Use small-scale decorative trees cultivated in containers to decorate rooms, corners and arch-ways.

A free-form Topiary, in the shape of a large basket

Caring for the Topiary

- Topiary looks best when groomed to exactly 2 in. of growth outside the frame. For best results prune, pinch and train regularly.

- Water or mist topiary regularly and evenly.

- Avoid excess water as this practice will result in root rot.

- Use black hairpins to pin growing vines in place.

- Feed monthly with water soluble plant food.

- Search for pests and eradicate them.

Bonsai

Bonsai is a garden art form which originated in Japan. The word Bonsai, means 'tree-in-a-pot.' It is an holistic art form comprised of horticulture, nature, aesthetics and Japanese art form. A tree planted in a pot becomes a bonsai after it has been pruned, shaped and trained into an aesthetically pleasing shape. Bonsai trees are ordinary trees which have been trained so as to produce the traditional growth forms. They are not dwarf trees. Bonsai is categorized in two groups; the Outdoor Bonsai and the Indoor Bonsai. Hardy trees are used for the Outdoor type, while the Indoor type is created from non-hardy trees and shrubs.

A Bonsai ; a-tree-in-a-pot, as seen at the Jamaica Horticultural Show, 2015

They require cool temperature, humidity and sunlight conditions. Some suitable plants are the Ficus Benjamina, Bougainvillea, Hibiscus, Umbrella Tree, Citrus, Cherry, Oak and the Poinciana. The time, patience and skill involved in producing this art form contributes to the high cost of the trees. Select a seedling or rooted cutting. When the main stem has reached the desired height pinch out the growing point of the upper side branches to encourage bushiness. Train the branches into attractive shapes by the use of stiff bonsai wire. Remove the wire before it becomes too tight and cuts into the bark of the tree. After 2 years, cut away 1/3rd of the roots and repot in a pot or on a bonsai tray. Remove some of the lower branches. Do this drastic pruning every 2 years. Grow Bonsai trees in a soil mixture that drains rapidly, so that roots are not allowed to be wet for long. Use rich, loose soil to prevent compaction. Moist air is essential and water is applied daily to satisfy the bonsai with high watering requirements. Keep your bonsai in semi-shade and feed with a foliar fertilizer every 4-6 weeks.

A Bonsai is often prized as a family heirloom.

Pollarding

Pollarding, is a specialized application that involves deep pruning to change the natural form of trees. Pollarding is done wherever trees lack the room to grow to their mature size. It involves the annual cutting back of new growth close to the main trunk without cutting into it. It is often done to prevent branches from tangling with overhead wires and other obstacles, to maintain trees at a predetermined size and to some degree prevent roots from growing into underground equipment. Pruning the canopy of the tree will also slow the growth of the roots and create a shorter tree with a uniform shape. It removes rotting or diseased branches to support the overall health of the tree, living and dead branches that could harm property and people, as well as expanded foliage for aesthetic, shade and pollution concerns. The best time to pollard a tree is in early spring, after the blooming season is over and before the tree has grown its new leaves. The arborist should cut back the new growth every year.

GROUND COVERS

Ground covers are low growing plants that spread quickly to form a dense carpet-like appearance. While grass is the best-known ground cover, it is not suited for all locations therefore, non-grass plants are used. Ground covers are not only beautiful but they can also be used to transform many problematic areas. There are four types of plants that are generally used as ground covers: **1.** Vines, which are woody plants with slender spreading stems. **2.** Herbaceous plants or non-wood plants. **3.**Low growing, spreading shrubs. **4 .** Moss of large, coarse species.

Ground covers are used to 'carpet' the ground under trees, along paths and driveways. These may be used around seating areas and in places that are generally suited for low growing plants. Your garden will be rendered incomplete without these ground covers. A ground cover planting project may become a significant maintenance problem if it is not managed properly. One way to achieve this is to get rid of all existing weeds before planting the ground covers. Allow the patch to stand for 4-6 weeks while you continue to dig and weed any new growth. If proper precautions are not followed the weeds will reduce the attractiveness of the ground cover or compete with it for resources such as water and nutrients.

All ground covers require maintenance. This is contradictory to the common perception that ground covers are non-maintenance plants. The grass that covers the lawns is a ground cover but may require more maintenance than many of the other ground covers. Evergreen ground covers require little care while others may need occasional pruning to confine them. Pruning older stems will allow young, vigorous and attractive foliage to grow. Some grow extremely fast and can become a nightmare, so select ground covers with caution. The leaves of ground covers are predominantly green but you will find some variegated, bronze, yellow, purple-bronze or silvery-white ones. Those that develop flowers often require more maintenance to keep them attractive. The Vinca (Periwinkle), is one such flowering ground cover which produces white, fuchsia or rose pink blooms.

You might have seen these ground covers around but never stopped to think that they could be used so effectively and that one could have gained so much pleasure from experimenting with them. Your increased awareness of their vibrant colours, aromas and textures will lead to new avenues. You may even begin to feel as if you are selecting and laying the carpet in the interior of your house.

Enhance the Garden with Ground Covers as these:

- Serve to highlight entrances, walkways, steps and driveways.

- Help to define space.

- Help to provide transition between the lawn and taller plants.

- Create various moods; small-leaves, smooth textured ground cover used in broad curved plantings can convey a feeling of spaciousness, while large leaves create a feeling of closeness.

- Reflect the garden style.

- Tidy the garden.

- Stimulate interest and bring unity to the ground, making them the unsung heroes.

- Cover the ground with a carpet of vegetation to prevent the germination of seeds.

- Protect the soil from erosion and water loss; particularly on slopes.

- Act as an insulating cover for the soil, keeping it cooler or warmer.

- Make a 'living' mulch that helps to build up humus level in the soil.

- Provide habitats and cover for beneficial insects and other predators.

- Provide us with other commodities like herbs, food and medicines.

- Can be used in fresh floral arrangements and in potpourri.

Vinca (Periwinkle)

GARDENING PASSION

Gorgeous Ground Covers in the Garden

Oxalis (Butterfly Plant)

Blue Gems

Creeping Persian Shield

Pink Rabbit Ears

Creeping Charley

Fittonia (Lace Plant)

Flame Violet

Pilea Beads

Grass

Dusty Joe

Ground Mint

Bronze Foxtail Grass

GARDEN PHOTOGRAPHY

Each garden has its own personality and capturing its characteristics is vital to portraying its personality. Some are adorned with fine topiary, elegant statuary, well-trimmed hedges and garden furniture. Some are decked in rolling lawns and lots of flora and fauna. With the fundamental knowledge of photography, you too can capture a wealth of photographic opportunities there in the garden. There are two types of garden photographs: one which gives an overall feeling of the garden and captures a sense of space and another which is focused more like a portrait than a landscape.

Four Photography Tips

1. *Keep your photographic apparatus simple.* A single camera with zoom lens will be sufficient. Digital cameras provide instant feedback. You can see them full-size as soon as you upload them to your computer. Remember, it is not the camera that makes beautiful images; it is the photographer.

2. *Choose the best time of day to shoot pictures*. Photography is 'writing with light' and finding the best light to show off your garden is the key to making beautiful pictures. A sunny garden is one of the trickiest places to take pictures. Shoot on a slightly overcast day, when the clouds diffuse the light, making it less intense. The best times are in the early morning or early evening when the light is softer and warmer. Choose a day when there is no breeze. Avoid shooting between 10.00 a.m. and 2 .00 p.m., this is when the overhead light is flat. If you are forced to shoot pictures during the sunlight, try to position yourself so that the sun hits your subject from the side. This will create a 3D effect.

3. *Fully engage your subject.* Single out your best specimen and give it your undivided attention. Timely observe the subject. You may see it differently when you are observing as a photographer and is seeking ways to emphasize it. Position yourself at the angle where you have the best vantage point. Get on your knees, shoot from the level of the objects or shoot from above with a bird's eye view. Fill the frame with the subject, look for a clean background and avoid any unwanted visual distractions. Look for repetition of shapes, reflections and designs in nature. Get close to your view, be a picture director.

4. *Variety remains the spice of life.* Put the garden into context by involving people and fitting objects or buildings. Shoot structures such as arches, bridges or hedges to frame subjects and draw the eye to a focal point. Look for extra garden features which enhance the landscape. Some of these are water fountains, birds splashing in the birdbath or the family pet barking up the tree at that frightened lizard.

Sunrise, the most intriguing part of a day when everything is waking up. Watch and witness the sun rising as it exudes energy that brings everything to life. The trees are stretching their sleepy limbs, the birds are leaving their cozy nests and nocturnal creatures are settling down to rest. Oh, what a wonder. !!! The rivers, the forests, the green mountains, living creatures and the flowers, all objects of nature stir at sunrise as part of the intriguing sunrise. See the misty rain lurking in the morning clouds.

Rise early and capture the intriguing sunrise

Beauty Abounds Everywhere

What does the cozy corner by your Royal Palm look like? Is it one of those hot spots?

Is it an explosion of mixed hues, perched on the edge of a skillfully organized floral chaos?

Would you like to hug that Palm in your wide clasp and feel the coolness of the trunk, the smoothness of its texture or bask in the high shade it provides? As you venture to take pictures you will be thrilled at the superb snapshots you can capture from high up, low down and from all angles.

If you are high-spirited, excited and a lover of warm colours this is the place where the

artistic side of you will find sheer pleasure.

Here, assorted hues, shades and tones of pink and green are highlighted by the soft glare of the sun nestled against the bright blue sky and

ruffled by the soft morning wind that flushes your immortal being with goose pimples.

Step back, look out, there are gorgeous photogenic scenes out there. Capture them..

Gorgeous !

A
Christmas
Palm
loaded
with
thousands
of seeds.

For many
months
the
gardens
will
be
illuminated
with
these
brightly
coloured
"pepper
lights."

GARDENING PASSION

Throw your head back, look up and do not miss the awesome combination of colours, hues and tints. See the various shades of green, bronze and yellow artistically etched against soft blue skies

With a great sense of balance the Sea Almond trees at the extreme ends seem to sandwich the Weeping Willow trees

The purple Allamanda, standing yards away from the Willow, seemingly stretches its vines to add colouor to the flushing greenery around while the Bird of Paradise supply broad, elongated foliage to bring solidity to the whole picture. Marvellous!!!!

The elegant June Rose, the powerful Royal Palm and the Weeping Willow whisper in the gentle breeze as the heavy morning clouds dissipate within the soft, blue skies

A few splashes of water from the mesmerizing waterfall won't stop my fellow garden enthusiast from finding the birds that insist on echoing their morning song

CHAPTER SEVEN

DECORATE WITH PLANTS

When words escape us, flowers speak." Anonymous

here is much pleasure in decorating the interior of the house using cut flowers and gorgeous potted plants. Use flowers to portray a feeling of luxury, to bring in an air of joy and to add the finishing flair to the décor. Use flowers to enhance good health, add fragrance, create light and reflect colours. Surely, the professional interior decorator will agree that the job is incomplete without flowers, as these also highlight focal points, express welcome to visitors or just quietly show off some radiance. Flowers are the perfect instruments to enhance the attractiveness of every room in the house. The choice of flowers can be used to evoke specific moods. So, the subtle blooms find their niche when the mood is calm and the strident ones are all aglow when the spirit is high. Flowers in the home can calm, excite, induce peace and refresh memories.

ENLIVEN THE LIVING ROOM

- The living room is the common room where the family members meet at the end of a tiresome day. Visitors are steered to the living room, hence this is the place for the showiest plants and blooms.

- Add flowers to bring positive emotional feelings to those who enter the living room, as flowers make the space more welcoming and create a sharing atmosphere.

- Consider the plants' lighting needs before you choose the location. They can be placed on a coffee table, end table, sofa table or on the floor. Choose a creeper or a vine and ensure that it is placed in an area where it has lots of room to grow. Hang it from the ceiling or from a hanging basket. Peace Lily, Ferns, Sansieveria, Philodendron and Orchids, all make the finest plants for the living room.

A theme depicted by flowers on the drapes

- Choose a classic floral theme for the living room. Be aware of the existing colour scheme and decorate the space accordingly. The theme chosen can be elegant, contemporary or even trendy. A theme is better used in a living room that is not already overcrowded with accessories.

- Place potted plants in classy, highly glazed pots and floral arrangements in lovely vases or containers. Use plants to highlight the crystal and china vases and platters.

- Arrange flowers and allow the blooms and the foliage to highlight the theme. Do not over decorate, as fewer flowers are better when decorating in a floral theme.

Blooms to complement the area

GARDENING PASSION

ADORN THE BATH ROOM

Bird of Paradise blooms decorate this cool bathroom. The graceful blooms will remain fresh for several days

Drape the bath surrounds with creepers , add coordinating colours

How very refreshing to enter a delicately perfumed bathroom and to be greeted by lively plants that literally smile at you. Here the plants seem so wide awake, fresh, clean and so happy. Allow them to embrace you. The design rules for the living room can be applied here, but the final touch is really the desire of the plant enthusiast. The bath's perimeter walls are most times too narrow to accommodate potted plants. However, if space is adequate, place selected plants there. Place plants on the shelf, window sill or in a corner on the vanity.

The colour scheme of your bathroom can be greatly enhanced by variegated greens and coloured foliage. These work magic with co-ordinating towels, rugs and drapes. Use warm colours and remember that white and yellow will add that extra light. The bathroom is the most suitable room in the house for the cultivation of exotic plants, such as the Anthurium, Caladium, Orchids, Bromeliads and other moisture loving plants. You may want to yield to the temptation to make a jungle of this room. This could be your chance to re-live those childhood experiences of swimming in the river and reaching to the edge with all its varied, lush green foliage. Well, go ahead and reminisce. Enjoy the luxury of your bathroom made elegant with freshly cut flowers and growing plants.

ADD ELEGANCE TO THE DINING ROOM

A low growing, flowering plant is ideal for the dining table. Failing this a low floral arrangement will do. Keep it low and spreading so it will not interfere with the conversation between folks on opposite sides of the table. Choose blooms and foliage carefully as diseased or dusty choices can be distasteful and

The pleasant fragrance of the Sage fills the air, while the warm colours of the Allamanda seek to indulge the guests in admirable conversation

embarrassing. Choose plants and blooms that are fragrantly pleasant, not pungent. A plain tablecloth will better highlight the colours. Display plants on a table or on a series of shelves to add an organic feel to the room. Add a specimen plant like a palm, a Zee Zee plant or a whispering bamboo on a pedestal, shelf, tabletop or sideboard and turn a plain, utilitarian room into a lush retreat. For a look of distinction accompany the plant display with fruits, spicy herbs or vegetables. Carved fruits or pumpkins enhanced with blooms, herbs, edible seeds and nuts will make a fine conversation piece in the dining room. This mouth-watering setting can also prove to be a boost to the appetite.

BRING AROMA AND COLOURS TO THE KITCHEN

Pick and bring in those juicy June plums for salads and juices

Ripe Gross Mitchell Bananas, Pineapple, Oranges, Plums and Limes Tangerines and Grapes

A platter of fresh fruits from the home garden

The kitchen has always been a popular and interesting place for plant life. It holds very moist air, the light is usually good and water is on hand. It is easy to pay 'snap attention' to the removal of dead foliage and flowers. The application of suitable mulch is made easy. Herbs, fruits, vegetables, along with nuts, seeds, spices and blooms befit the décor of the kitchen. Display them on suitable trays, in shallow baskets or on the countertops. Add a few bottles of the mellow home-made wines or colourful pickles to the display. Bring in the specimen plants and position them with interest. Do not forget those of the philodendron family as some will drape, climb or trail at your guidance and help to soften those hard lines in your kitchen.

The kitchen is the most frequently used space in the house. Family members roam throughout it all day. Visitors are often entertained there and are served invigorating teas from the herbs growing in pots within arm's reach. What will you serve today? Is it the Lemon Grass, the Peppermint, the Black Mint or is it a combination of all these herbs? With the many fruits displayed around, how about a quick fruit plate? Keep the kitchen energized with the aroma of fresh herbs, brewing teas, spices, blooms and fruits.

PLACE PLANTS IN THE BEDROOM

Benefit from restful sleep and ward off health problems attributed to pollutants by embellishing the bedroom space with house plants. Viruses, mould, dust mites, bacteria and mildew are built up when bedroom windows and doors are kept tightly closed. During the photosynthesis and respiratory processes plants release moisture which increases humidity and decreases the incidence of dry skin, colds, sore throats and dry coughs. House plants absorb poisonous toxins through their leaves, making them a smart choice for the bedroom. Use these living organisms to interact with your body, mind and home in ways that enhance the quality of life.

Plants such as the Peace lily, Golden Pothos, Aloe vera, Philodendron and Orchids are known to remove chemicals. Use them to improve the air quality in the bedroom by acting as botanical filters and providing fresh, clean air while you sleep. Add real growing plants with a subtle aroma and wake up feeling healed and rejuvenated. This 'outdoors' sleeping environment will keep you forever young. This is an exciting way to utilize your vanity mirror is as a multiplier. Anything placed close to a mirror appears to have twice the mass, so a potted plant or a floral arrangement placed on the dressing table will take on a grandeur sense. All sides of the plant will be now exposed so there is no backside.

Select plants with colourful foliage to enhance the décor

Multiply your blooms by playing

tricks with the mirror

DECORATE THE PATIO AT RANDOM

The patio is unique. It fosters an illusion of being outdoors. Here you have the beauty of your natural surroundings coupled with furnishing and accessories that supply the comfort of an indoor room. This indoor and outdoor juxtaposition allows you the freedom to decorate the patio to suit your whims and fancies. You may be tempted to convert and christen it as "the garden room", " sun room" or "lounge." The important idea is that it is inviting, fabulous and functional. Create a blissful indoor garden using the tropical beauties that could not have displayed their exotic blooms under the in-house conditions. Place potted plants of various sizes in nice containers around the perimeter of the patio area, suspend plants in hanging baskets and create a vertical garden. Cover the floor with canvas or rugs and allow your guests to go barefooted and enjoy the outdoors, while adding style and flair in an unobtrusive manner. Artwork is not restricted to indoors anymore. Outdoor canvas art using long-lasting, waterproof materials are perfect to decorate the wall. Add statues, waterfalls or wall fountains. These make interesting focal points on a patio but their sizes should be in balance with the size of the patio. A low table surrounded by cushions or bean bags can make a great games and craft area. Choose furniture with waterproof surfaces to ensure that everything is easy to clean after a project or after a party.

Install suitable lighting and make the patio ready for evening parties. Place comfortable chairs, recliners, footrests or hammocks. Place comfortable cushions on the reclining chair and bask in the sun; which is vital for health, beauty and longevity. The privacy of your lounge allows you to sunbathe, while you listen to the orchestra provided by the chirping birds in the garden. If you need to sun gaze, do so right after sunrise or before sunset as other times could be dangerous for the eyes. Relax and read the newspapers or the Health, Home and Garden Jamaican magazine. Take a snooze, write a letter, converse on your mobile phone or have a cup of invigorating herbal tea. Enjoy the company of your canine pets, the pretty birds in their cage or your friendly fish in the nearby aquarium. Here is a whole realm of new exciting gardening experiences. Go wild and enjoy the adulation.

THE PRINCIPLES OF ARRANGING FLOWERS

- **Unity** is achieved when the flowers chosen for the arrangement complement each other in colour, shape and proportion.

- **Balance** is achieved when the arrangement is physically balanced. Symmetrical designs are balanced when it is the same on either side of the centre. Asymmetrical designs are achieved when one side is longer or higher than the other.

- **Proportion** is achieved when there is a balance between the flowers, the container and the surroundings in which the arrangement is placed.

- **Focal point** is achieved by placing the largest, darkest and most flowers in the centre of the arrangement. Round arrangements do not have a focal point.
  Harmony is achieved when the items used harmonize and complement one another.

- **Radiation** is achieved when all the flower stems are radiating from one point in the arrangement.

- **Repetition** is achieved when colours or elements are repeated.
  Depth is achieved by determining the height and width of the arrangement.

- **Rhythm** is achieved by spacing flowers at regular intervals in the arrangement.
  Transition is achieved by using filler flowers to transition from large to small flowers.

Making the Arrangement
1. Wash or sterilize the cutting tools and the container.

2. Select stems which are green, smooth and freshly cut; stems and buds should be firm.

3. Remove leaves that will fall below the water line as these will rot. Make a fresh cut on stems while they are under water, this should be done every other day when the water is changed.

4. Always cut stems on an angle, this allows water to be drawn up to the head of the flower.

- Two inches of water in the container will supply sufficient moisture. Add water daily to maintain the water level and add a dash of household bleach to keep it nice and fresh.

- Interesting containers such as drinking glasses, wine decanters or carafes, pitchers and bottles can be improvised as interesting vases.

- Fix flowers in the vase to create the arrangement you desire.

- Keep cut flowers fresh by protecting them from direct sunlight and draughts.

- Use preservative that comes with the flowers or make your own.

- Remove blossoms and foliage that have faded, this will preserve the fresher flowers and improve the overall appearance of the arrangement.

Selecting Containers

A very important element in a floral arrangement is the container. It should be relevant in colour, size, style and texture. Reach for the canisters, glassware, perfume bottles, wine bottles, vintage pitchers, tea cups, tea pots and tins and put them to work for you. Use those large conch shells, driftwood and bamboo joints too.

Vases: Bud vases are usually taller with a narrow opening. Taller vases with wider openings allow for more flowers and for mixed arrangements. Vases are usually made of glass, ceramic or plastic. These may be opaque or clear and lend themselves to casual, freeform or formal designs.

Basic containers: These are obtainable in plastic, glass, ceramic, bamboo and wicker.

Baskets: Baskets are usually made from organic materials such as wicker, bamboo, thatch or straw. These may be painted or used in their natural form. Conceal a small pot in one of these baskets; which may be designed with or without handles.

Ceramic: Ceramic containers are made with various decorative accents that often attribute to special sentiments. Mugs are popular items found in this group.

Tools For Floral Arrangements

Floral Foam

Floral Foam or Oasis: This is available in blocks that can be cut to the desired size. It is used to hold and provide water for the flowers in the arrangement. Soak thoroughly in water before use.

Wire Mesh

Wire Mesh Netting /Chicken Wire: This is usually available in 1 in. mesh. It is often used over floral foam in large arrangements. It provides structural support for heavier stems.

Dried Foam

Dried Foam: This is made primarily for use with silk and dried materials. It is sold in blocks or sheets. It is attached to the container with florist glue.

Needle Point Holders

Needle Point Holder: A needlepoint holder, 'frog,' or Kenzan is a metal-based object with needle-like prongs projecting up from the base. It is used to hold flowers in the arrangement. Cut the flower stems at an angle. Fasten flower stems carefully. These are best used for Ikebana arrangements or are placed at the bottom of a vase or container.

Floral Tape

Floral Tape Without Adhesive: A self-sealing wrap for covering stems or wires and for fastening or attaching novelty items.

Floral Tape with Adhesive: This is used to secure floral foam to a container. Crisscross it above the foam and fasten it on the vase. It adheres to clean, dry surfaces and will remain in place even after getting wet.

Tape with adhesive

Florist Wire: This green-coated wire is a staple for floral designs. It is available in different sizes and is used to lengthen, curve or strengthen stems. The higher the gauge number the more flexible or thinner is the wire.

Florist Wire

GARDENING PASSION

Water tubes

Greening Pins

Knife

Wire Cutter

Ribbon Shear

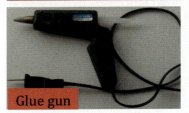
Glue gun

Secateurs

Water tubes: These are plastic tubes used to hold water. These are inserted directly into floral foam or taped to wooden picks for additional height. Camouflage them in the arrangements. Water should be added daily. Some lipstick covers make fine water tubes.

Greening Pins: These are like hairpins with flat tops and are used to attach moss, foliage or ribbons to the design. These are often used in silk or dried arrangements.

Knife: An all-purpose knife is handy. It makes the cutting and shaping of the oasis to the shape of the vase quite easy.

Wire Snips or cutters: Utility snips are used for shortening wire lengths. They can be used to cut through a large quantity of wire easily. Use wire snips to cut mesh or thick plastic stems.

Ribbon Shears: Shears or scissors are used for cutting ribbons, trimming foliage or for any other uses where a clean, sharp cutting tool is needed.

Glue gun: A hot glue gun is an essential tool in silk or dried arrangement. This should be used with utmost care to avoid burns. Keep a first aid kit handy.

Secateurs: Shears are used for cutting stems. This is the most important tool a florist owns, since all flower stems must be cut before being placed into an arrangement.

Selecting Vases

Size: The size of the opening will determine the number of stems that will fill the container.

Shape: This should flow with the arrangement to create harmony.

Style: The container should coordinate with the theme of the arrangement.

Texture: This should complement the materials used in the design.

Colour: The colour of the container should blend with the design or become part of the focal point.

Blending vase with blooms

Arranging Flowers in a Vase

Vase arrangements are flowers loosely arranged in a vase without mechanical support. Bud vases for single stems are usually made of glass, crystal, porcelain or ceramic and are generally tall and narrow. A bud vase arrangement of one type of flowers has a more structured design style than a large vase of mixed flowers. Larger vases are meant to hold many stems of flowers.

The Magic of Vases

Clear vases are usually transparent or translucent and allow you to see all the contents in them. They are elegant. Maybe you would like to use some attention-grabbing fillers such as river stones, beads, pebbles, shells, glass chips, gems or pearls. They allow you to have fun with the blooms, their stems and their roots and also to express your creativity without fear. Clear vases are suitable for lilies. All blooms, foliage and stems seem comfortable in them. Fish bowls, vegetable bowls and bubble ball vases are suitable.

Crystal vase

Ensure that the water in the clear vase is changed every other day so as to keep it pristine at all times. Rid the vase of any deposit by washing in clean soapy water. Highlight this arrangement and double the pleasure by setting the vase on a clear mirror.

Crystal Vases

These are usually etched with classy designs that catch the light in wondrous ways, bending it and casting the beams throughout the room. These transparent vases are definitely stylish and will suit the interior of any household; be it traditional or contemporary. They make charming gifts that aught to be treasured and kept as family heirlooms.

Opaque Vases and Platters

These also make envied home décor items that are treasured for generations. These are excellent for adding a rich and solid feel to the décor and will reflect a graceful antique style that aught to attract lots of attention. This is an elegant way to display fresh or dried floral arrangements.

A clear vase with floating hibiscus blooms placed on a mirror

On their own they add that touch of elegance and sophistication and offer more freedom as to the types of flowers or decorative materials you put in them.

Platters

FLORAL DESIGNING TECHNIQUES

Round Arrangements

Round arrangements are referred to as mounds and are suitable for almost any occasion. These are ideally used as centrepieces and should be low and not obstructive. Candles make fine accessories to these arrangements.

Morning Glory blooms

Design Tips

The arrangement should radiate from the centre of the container as the round arrangement does not carry a focal point.

- Flowers may be of one colour only. (Monochromatic)

- Foliage or other greenery can be used as a filler.

- Non-fresh items can be added to the round arrangement. Live the season as you add small balloons, candles, dried branches, ribbons and other trims.

- Arrange in a shallow bowl or round basket.

Centrepiece Arrangements

Centrepiece arrangements are often misconstrued as being only round arrangements. These may however be rectangular or square. They should be low and horizontal so that they facilitate and not obstruct the view, nor interrupt the conversation.

A centrepiece

Design Tips

The centrepiece design is ideal for formal settings, dining tables and boardrooms. These may be done as monochromes and are impressive when done in bright, bold colours. Selected dried material can enhance these arrangements.

Ikebana loves space, height and outreach

Ikebana : The Oriental Way

Think oriental and the Ikebana design comes to mind. This design loves space, height, depth and outreach. The elements of heaven, man and earth give this arrangement feelings of peace and expressions of movement. Use together, blooms, branches, foliage, stones and dried organic material to carry out the theme.

Design Tips

- Keep the design open.
- Use one or two varieties of flowers to maximize the effect.
- Use a shallow container.
- Use seasonal elements to create the design.
- A kenzan or "frog" is essential in this design. This Japanese art form is meant to be free, creative and not confined to flowers and foliage, therefore any material can be used.

Caring for the Fresh, Floral Arrangement

- Avoid placing the finished arrangement in the sun, near sources of heat or in the draught. These conditions can cause pre-mature wilting.

- Lightly spray the arrangement with clean, clear water from time to time. Do not spray near furniture or near electrical appliances.

- Avoid placing arrangement on top of working electrical appliances.

- If the arrangement is done in a vase, ensure that you use of floral preservatives.

Simply reach for the foliage and blooms and create a pleasing arrangement

- Cut off the spent blooms and dry leaves; this will help to preserve the flowers.

- The stems of flowers that have been placed in a vase should be cut every 1-2 days to promote the intake of water. Use this opportunity to change the preservative solution and to wash the vase. Make your preservative by adding 2 tablespoons lemon juice or lime juice, 1 tablespoon sugar and 1/2 teaspoon bleach to 1 gallon water.

- If you use an oasis ensure that it does not dry out.

- Flowers should not be placed near fruits or vegetables in the refrigerator. Some of these food items give off ethylene gas, which will affect the life of the flowers. Put the container with flowers in an airtight plastic bag and add some wet towels to provide humidity. Store on the top shelf.

Gorgeous Foliage Used In Floral Arrangements

Exotic leaves of the Fish Tail Palm from the Interest group

Foliage has often been seen as simply leaves, so very little importance is placed on them. These are merely used as fillers and have not been recognized for their real beauty, form and purpose. Today, foliage has stepped forward and has assumed a pivotal position in the art of floral design. Exotic leaves, rosettes, variegated grasses and vines are being used in a number of original ways. Variegated foliage offers patterns not only in hues of greens but in white, gold, red, yellow and bronze. The patterned foliage is often splashed, tinged, striped, dotted and blotted to create astounding effects. Foliage is classified in four groups; *Line foliage, Mass foliage, Filler foliage and Interest foliage.*

Line foliage is further divided into two groups, which helps to identify them. In the Narrow linear group are narrow leaf plants, some of which are the Iris, Sansevieria and Daffodil. The Broad linear can be found in the Dracaena, Bird of Paradise and Cannas. **Mass foliage** is used to tie a design together, to add weight and to create balance. These are broad, short leaves, used as a backdrop. Look among the Hostas and the Pothos for this category. **Filler foliage** is used to fill spaces, to make backdrop and to increase the depth in an arrangement. Look among the many ferns for this very impressive group. **Interest foliage** will capture the interest of the audience. This group consists of big and bold leaves with distinctive shapes and brilliant colours. Find these among the Crotons, Philodendron and Palms.

Decorative grass (Carex morrowii) "Variegata" from the narrow linear group

GARDENING PASSION

Lattice design on top of an earthenware jar

Utilizing Dried Flowers

You too can produce aesthetically pleasing dried floral arrangement without the traditional vase, oasis or kenzan. Look around for any container with a wide mouth. Put in some clean, dry sand or pebbles to occupy 4-6 inches of the base. Use some strong, clear tape to create a lattice across the top. This will keep the flowers evenly spaced, while the sand helps to hold the stems in place. The container can be a large mug, a bucket, a keg, an antique jar or a hollow chunk of wood.

Design Tips

Include branches, flowers, foliage, drift wood and moss

1. Select the appropriate size, colour and style container.
2. Note the space in which the arrangement will be placed.
3. If the container is shallow place some marbles, pebbles, shells or layers of moss to conceal the foam and to weight the container down.
4. Dried flowers are very light, so the deep container should be weighed down to provide stability.
5. If necessary lengthen stems by using wire or wooden picks.
6. Select dried flowers and foliage of varying shapes, colours and textures for a more visually appealing creation.
7. Arrange the flowers in a natural manner and ensure that the colours are evenly distributed.
8. Allow adequate space between the flowers.
9. Pep up an arrangement by adding plant materials by applying coat of acrylic spray to revitalize the sheen and by using a hair dryer set on low to blow off dust that might have accumulated on them.

Those bigger, coarser, dried botanicals make wonderful, dried arrangements too. Don't throw them out

Potpourri

Potpourri is the combination of dried botanicals with fixative to hold the aroma and perfume oils to enhance the aroma. Whole or crushed spices; cinnamon sticks, nutmeg and cloves may also be added. Potpourri is a simple way to capture the essence of your garden This can reach all the friends and family members who were not there to enjoy the fresh aroma.

Gather the Ingredients

A long list comprising Roses, Wild hops, Marigold, Yucca, Dracaena and Sansevieria blooms, pods, cones, berries, roots, seeds, nuts, grass, mints, pimento, sage and orange peel are all botanicals that can be collected for this project. Reap and handle flowers and herbs carefully as bruising will cause the loss of essential oils and perfumes. Collect botanicals in the early morning after the dew has dried off. Choose fresh, open blooms and clean healthy plants. Botanicals shrink, so collect four times the amount required. These may be collected over a period to allow for a variety of colours, textures and aroma.

Drying The Ingredients

Reap botanicals and tie their stems and hang these upside down or spread leaves out in thin layers and dry in a warm, dry place with ample air circulation. Flowers and leaves are dry when they feel slightly brittle. If over dry they will lose all their oil and crumble easily.

Dried arrangement

Making Potpourri   Select dried botanicals.

- Mix them together to create the perfect texture.

- Place some Fiber fix in a glass or bowl.

- Create a spray made with essential oils and label it.

- Add scented oils or perfume to fiber mix.

- Cover and allow the oil to soak in for 4 hours.

- Stir this into a botanical blend. Mix well.

- Pour the batch into a large paper bag to blend.

- Fasten bag with clips or clothes pins and shake daily.

Dried red roses

After 7 days the potpourri is ready to be packaged in small bags as gifts or to be displayed in dishes. Enclose a packet of silica gel in every pound of potpourri to absorb any moisture and to prevent mould or mildew. Potpourri has a wonderfully uplifting scent that helps to overcome stale and unpleasant smell in an enclosed area. Refresh your potpourri to avoid replacing it. Use the spray to refresh old potpourri that has lost its scent. The spray can also double as an air and linen freshener.

Dried stalks of the Princess flowers

Glass bowl filled with potpourri

CHAPTER EIGHT

ENHANCE YOUR GARDEN

Gardening and laughing are two of the best things in life you can do to promote good health and a sense of well-being."

Anonymous

Unlike the privacy of the space on the inside of the house, the outside is totally exposed to the scrutiny of the observant public. This being so, one can create a beautiful and inviting exterior and even double the usable outdoor space. The inside space is usually lavishly furnished for utmost comfort. There are rugs covering the floor, paintings and pictures of interest hanging on the walls, exotic perfumed blooms displayed in nice vases and a range of tactical lighting to complete the sophisticated decor. Scattered around are a number of hand crafted embellishments and souvenirs collected to give that touch of class.

Gardens and garden settings are really the defining aspect of the overall appearance of your home. Gardens are not just trees and flowers carefully designed and tended, they are really signs of the designer's personality. Your garden reflects you; hence gardeners make that concerted effort to use the garden to add personality, character and value to their homes. Adorn the landscape with ornamental trees, lush lawns and vibrant blooms. The addition of long-lasting garden furniture and fixtures will serve to enhance the comfort and help to provide the sought after ambience. Accessories including lawn umbrellas, plant stands, antique ceramic jars and large pots are also on the list. The old cartwheel, bridges over man-made streams and additional water features are befitting too. The birdbath, the trellis and the gazebo are often included in the gardens. When you seek to retreat from the frantic pace of modern life, your garden is the place that offers peace and quietude. Here, as in the interior of the house, you can relax and unwind in style and comfort while enjoying the fresh, clean air and fine weather.

INCLUDE WATER FEATURES

Enrich your garden with water features and enjoy the outdoor living space. These may be comprised of unusual containers with water, water falls and classical fountains. These features enhance the garden and create a visual and acoustic appeal. The sound of whirling or cascading water promotes relaxation and adds a dramatic element to the garden. I recently installed a water fountain at the entrance of my garden and realized that I had opened the door to a new and enchanting world. Its presence mesmerizes my senses, enriches the garden's design and excites my garden visitors.

Birdbath

Would you like to see and hear those feathered friends in your garden? Then it is high time to install a birdbath. When the weather is hot birds come along, frolic and drink water from the birdbath. This is the simplest type of water feature for the garden and it can be made ready and installed within a few minutes. Position the birdbath in a sunny spot. Give yourself the opportunity to see the birds jostle to bathe, to have a drink or just to perch on the rim of the bath. The birdbath attracts birds. A large bowl between 4-6 in. deep, a large saucers or a wide, shallow basin filled with water and raised on wooden blocks makes a fine

This satellite dish has been improvised to serve as a dual purpose water feature; a reflecting pond, as well as a birdbath

birdbath. Place this in a secluded and sunny spot and await the eager birds. Birds like warm and moving water so you can customize your birdbath with drippers. A well maintained, clean bath will ensure a year-round, energized and flirtatious landscape. There will be much frolic that one may become uncertain whether or not the birds are having fun or fighting.

Container water gardens can be made of any water-tight container. Here you can include aquatic plants, fish and water snails.

Tabletop fountains add a subtle charm to the garden, the home or office and serve as a natural humidifier. Many people enjoy the wonderful, relaxing sound of this small gadget.

A garden wall fountain is suitable for a small space. Some are made with a floor base and are placed against a wall, others are stand-alone fittings. This can be used indoors or outdoors

A reflection or reflecting pool consists of a shallow pool of water, undisturbed by water pumps.

Simple sprays can trickle, shoot or gush water in or out of a pool and promote a lot of fun.

Trickling streams connect one pond to another. Meander shallow streams in circles around trees or create them along walkways. Keep streams natural by using assorted size rocks. Select a pump that will pump the volume of water you require. A small pump will send a drizzle of water over the falls or down the stream.

A swimming pool to be used for swimming or water-based recreation. Chemical disinfectants such as chlorine, an acid for ph balance and additional filters are often used to prevent the growth of bacteria, viruses, algae and insect larvae.

A water fountain is capable of transforming ordinary gardens into classy, sophisticated ones. This is usually a statue or a tiered structure that water is pumped through and allowed to cascade into a container. Most fountains are self contained; the water is recycled from a pond. These fountains work magic on the ears and on your the eyes too. They bring the freshness of nature into your space. A water fountain is a popular garden amenity.

Install a Water Fountain

Procure necessary supplies: You need a fountain and its attachments, tools, building materials, a submersible pump, electrical and plumbing supplies.

An active three tiered water fountain

- **Placement:** Choose the ideal location so that it can be viewed and appreciated from the porch or as a focal point in the landscape.

- **Avoid Trees:** The leaves falling in the pond can decay and clog the pumps and filters. Be reminded that growing tree roots can damage the pond from underground.

- **Ensure Accessibility To Water:** The pond will most likely be filled with tap water and will occasionally need topping up when the water level gets low due to evaporation. An accessible water source is mandatory.

- **Ensure Accessibility to Electricity:** An electrical submergible pump which is used to re-circulate the water requires a normal household circuit supply.

- **Special Regulations:** Some municipalities have special ordinances that effect the location of pools, ponds, fencing etc. Consult with the local officials for any such guidelines.

- **Depth of Pond:** It is recommended that the depth does not exceed 24 in.

- **Ensure Accurate and Level Measurements:** The beauty of the waterfall lies in the equal distributed flow of water from all angles. Each tier should be installed and allowed to dry before the other tier is installed as even a slight wind can adjust the level of each tier during installation.

GARDEN ACCESSORIES

Install elaborate seating

Seating   Seating is an important element in the garden and it is incomplete without seating. Sitting outdoors is an excellent reason for having a garden. It allows you to wine and dine outdoors, while it creates a pleasant atmosphere in which to entertain. In the garden, you are more inclined to relax, read, meditate or just close your eyes and be entertained by the birds.

A wide variety of outdoor seating is available and is designed to suit your budget. Some are made of aluminium, steel, metal, plastic or wood. Select that which will fit your budget or you may choose to construct your own. Ensure that these are practical, elegant and durable. Suitable garden seating include:

- Tree trunks
- Hunks of wood
- Hammocks
- Flat stones
- Lounge chairs
- Reclining chairs

Sitting low on a flat stone; for the fun of it

A greenhouse , a part of the garden settings

The greenhouse, the garden room, or the conservatory are rooms designed mainly for the comfort of your shade-loving plants. Shade cloth for the roof will protect the delicate foliage from the harsh sun and the perforated walls will provide adequate ventilation. Avoid using polished furniture. Plastic, cane or rust-proof metal is best suited for this damp atmosphere. Cover sections of the floor with gravel.

Lawn umbrellas are very becoming. These add shade, character and flair to your surroundings. The most interesting gardens are those with much shade.

Fences are used as borders or to define boundaries. Shrub, wooden, chain linked or picket fences transform the appearance of the surroundings and provide security. Traditional fences are made of wood and finished with paint or polish. Contemporary fencing can now be procured in plastic or fiberglass.

Gates give the entrance an impressive, unique look. Gates are fashioned from wrought

A white wooden ranch-style fence

iron, aluminium and treated lumber. Wrought iron gates are simple to maintain. The natural look and rugged strength of wood is often the preferred choice. You may mount the name of your dwelling and the street number on your gate.

A metal gate

Garden Features 1. Accent your entrance and patio.   **2.** Create traffic barriers.

3. Integrate the architecture with the landscape.   **4.** Enhance and add class to the surroundings.

5. Weave exotic themes or décor in your landscape. **6.** Add design features to the landscape.

7. Conceal unsightly areas.   **8.** Some features often used or found in the garden are heirlooms.

Genuine clay jars have provided cool drinking water for many generations. These have been replaced by the grand refrigerator. What better way to preserve and treasure such an invaluable piece of family heirloom than to blend it into the home or garden décor?

Bricks are full of character and give a sculptured effect in the garden. They make great garden features and are capable of standing alone or combined with other features. They outlast wood, add a hard edge of great contrast to the garden's soft greenery and flowers and are energizing and pleasing. Use bricks to highlight your entrance and patio.

Garden feature suitable
for your décor

A wheel

Not a real snake; a piece of driftwood mounted on a flat stone

Antique Clay jar

Bricks

Stones In The Garden

Integrate some stones into the landscape and add depth, texture, seating and even a sculptural element. Stones can successfully improve the look of your landscape, so do not throw them out. It is quite economical to use stones. For more travelling fun you can collect interesting stones as you holiday in the countryside and on the sea coast. Stones are heavy; handle them with utmost care. Stones provide ideal hiding places for spiders, ants, worms and snakes, so venture carefully into their space. The types of stones you find in your environment depend on the geology.

Stones are the most sturdy of all garden materials, they are everlasting. Use these aesthetically designed elements for creating paths, terraces, accents and walls. They are vital in the rock and water gardens where they can be used to edge a pool or stream. Stones may be cut and shaped to your liking. Flagstones are often man-made and are used as pavers and stepping stones.

A gnarled stone; securely mounted to create a masterpiece

River stones

Honey comb rocks

Sea Treasures

Sea coral bears the rather beautiful nick-name of "Sea's Garden." Sea coral forms in warm waters from the skeletons of marine animals that live together in groups. They come in yellow, orange, red, purple and white. Their varied shapes include branching, fan-shaped and feather-shaped. Find these treasures washed up on the nearby beach.

Sea coral

GARDENING PASSION

Naturally sculptured driftwood

Walking the seashores and hunting for sea treasures such as driftwood is one pastime that is enjoyed by everyone. Driftwood, which may be described as gnarled nature's sculpture, is full of intriguing surprises. Pick up every piece you find, as you may be able to use them as is or you may construct images from a combination of pieces. You may drill holes to accommodate fittings to make them into figures that can be displayed around the house, on the patio and in the garden. A collection can be used to create interesting borders for the flower garden. Sea treasures such as the sea fans often find their way in the garden as interesting collectables. Take a microscopic look at the Sea Fan and observe the intricate colouration. Use them to enhance the cactus, rock and water gardens.

Seashells make a one–of-a-kind handcraft art. Nature has already sculpted, painted and polished them. Display them in the house or in the garden to brighten up any area and to add colour, interest and texture. Use them as containers or to accentuate the plant display. Use conch shells to grow small plants as the roots will travel through to the inner shell. Use shells to make borders, but protect them from the immediate soil which can smudge the highly polished finish. Find and use the large flat clamp shells as decorated mulch.

Malik is fascinated by the many wonders of Jamaica. Now he listens for the intriguing sound of the sea waves

Ornaments

Garden ornaments can be shifted from place to place to make their contribution to the aesthetics and theme. Many people like to bring back souvenirs from their vacations; maybe your desire is to bring back garden ornaments. Bring these in and add a sense of serenity to the garden décor. Interesting bottles, antiques and household crockery, all make suitable ornaments for the garden. Use ornaments to attract the attention of wild life. Use a fresh coat of paint to bring new life even to old garden ornaments.

Revamp the faded flamingo

This feature is appropriately placed by the water

Garden art

Use outdoor fabric for table covers

Soft Furnishings

The type of soft furnishing you choose will tell a lot about your personality. Use special outdoor fabrics (sunbrella) for drapes, cushions, upholstering, framed wall hangings and some dazzling table covers. Select brightly coloured fabric to suit the season or the theme. Add bright, assorted cushions and cast a whimsical flair of comfort in the garden and its surroundings. Cover floors with outdoor carpet.

Bright colours for cushions

ATTRACT WILDLIFE

Butterflies Butterflies, the "Wings of Grace" need the sun them warm, so plant your butterfly garden in a sunny location. They also prefer a wind free area where they won't be constantly fighting the wind. Place a few flat stones in the sunny spot so that the butterflies can take a break while warming up. Butterflies need water. Make a mud puddle or place a shallow container with some flat stones in it. Add some water for them. The stones should extend above the water level, allowing butterflies to drink without to keep getting wet. Butterflies are particularly attracted to coloured blooms. Different species usually prefer different flowers, but they will generally feed on many types of flowers. It is good to include the sunflower, marigold and zinnias. They also enjoy a meal of over-ripe fruits. Let

Butterfly sp.

Butterfly sp.

us not get too annoyed as the butterflies begin their life cycle in your gardens. Allow for the damaged leaves and wait to be compensated by the swarm of colourful butterflies that will emerge after six weeks. Take a keen look at the remarkable transformation that takes place there in the garden.

Stage 1.   Butterflies lay eggs on the underside of leaves.

Stage 2.   The eggs develop into larvae. (caterpillar) These devour lots of juicy leaves.

Stage 3.   Caterpillar becomes a pupa. (chrysalis) It does not eat but secures a sheltered environment. It frequently hangs its camouflaged self from the host leaf.

Stage 4.   A pupa develops into a beautiful butterfly.

"Pretty, pretty butterfly, what you do all day, Play among the sunny flowers, nothing to do but play, Nothing to do but play, All the live-long day, Fly butterfly, fly butterfly, Don't waste your time away".

Be Prepared For The Birds

As you proceed with that concerted effort to attract birds and have them loiter in your garden, you should be cognizant of their three basic requirements; that of food, shelter and water. This being so, an assortment of plants that provide seeds, berries, nuts and other food throughout the year should be included. Organic gardening entices birds in the garden. This garden is teeming with insects, worms, bugs and other organisms that birds enjoy. So, while they are adding life to the garden they are also controlling garden pests and insects. Sacrifice an area of the landscape that will meet the requirement of some of these birds.

A Bird House

Some birds love what is defined as an unkempt space with rotted trees and lots of mulch. This is where you will pile large, dry branches, standing dead trees and tree stumps. These make excellent bird attractors as they provide food in the form of insects, larvae as well as nesting homes for woodpeckers and other cavity-nesting birds. Avoid littering the ground with food, as this will attract the unwanted visitors like rats and ants. Hang bird feeds and supply the grains. You may be lucky to get a visit from the indigenous National Bird of Jamaica, the "Hummingbird," also known as the "Doctor Bird". They display beautiful feathers of iridescent colours; a characteristic that belongs only to that bird family. It is interesting to note that the mature male has two long feathers which stream behind him when he flies. Next to the outermost feathers on each side of the male's tail are 6 or 7 in. long feathers. These feathers make a humming sound, hence its name. You may also be visited by the Jamaican black birds, known as the smartest birds in the world. Jamaica has eight different species of birds that are black in colour; most of which are commonly called 'black birds'.

The long-legged and graceful heron

Pigeons are intelligent birds. They are tame and befriend the people they meet in the environment that they often adopt. They are often seen in large flocks of 50 or more birds.

The tame pigeons

They have excellent hearing abilities which makes them capable of detecting and immediately reacting to sounds. Seeds and fruits form a major component of their diets hence their presence in fruits trees growing in the home gardens. They are up with the sun so that will catch the worm,

Pond Turtles The pond sliders are semi–aquatic turtles. They are omnivorous, they love the garden environment and they make fine pets. They can live for more than 60 years and grow up to 12 in. in diameter. Feed them with bite-size pieces of vegetables and fruits such as ripe bananas and apples. Place their food on a rock and they will haul the food into the water. Pond turtles relish earth worms and crickets and you can watch them fight over a piece of sausage. Use a pond filter to keep the quiet pond clean. Fence them in to ensure their safety; if allowed, they will crawl out.

Attempting a quick get-away

The Busy Bee

Pollination at its best

The Busy Bee Gardens need bees. Without these pollinators there would be a limited supply of fruits, flowers and vegetables. They are tiny, beautiful and busy but they are not as quiet as the butterflies. They hum and we are compelled to listen, but do you want to hear that hum or is it too close for comfort? There is no need to be so scared of them as nearly all species of bees are gentle. Their aim is not to sting, they simply are on their search for pollen and nectar.

Bees prefer a bee-friendly garden with a large collection of flowers where they can find plenty of pollen and nectar to make honey. Single petal blooms attract the bee more than double petal blooms, because the inner parts of the single petal flowers are easier to access. Cultivate blooms of blue, yellow, purple and lavender during the four seasons, so that they will not have a reason to leave your garden. Bees need water; create puddles by filling shallow containers with sand and water.

The Soldier Crab The Caribbean terrestrial hermit crab is best known as the soldier crab. They are very smart and quite sensitive to the presence of anyone around. When threatened or startled they take quick refuge in the seemingly heavy shell they carry around. These crabs changing into larger shells as they grow. As children we timidly collected and kept them as scary pets, until they struggled their way out of the container and made good their escape. These crabs may be as small as a thimble or as big as a baseball. They too are omnivorous, they visit the gardens and will devour most of what they are find.

Soldier crab

GARDENING PASSION

NIGHT-TIME IN THE GARDEN

"I love the smell of flowers after dark; you get hold of their souls then." **Anonymous**

Flowers and Fragrances in the Night Garden

Most plant enthusiasts spend lots of time in the garden during the day but at nightfall they close their doors to the garden and unwittingly deny themselves the pleasures of sharing the activities that take place out there at nights. They miss the garden's enormous potential as a twilight wonderland. Sit out in the garden at nights, feel the soft breeze as it glides against your cheeks and inhale the smell of those wonderfully fragrant blooms, herbs and vegetables as they release appealing fragrances. Flowers that are most fragrant during the day are brightly coloured and are primarily visited by bees, butterflies, wasps, flies and beetles. There are many flowers that bloom only after the sun goes down infusing the air with a variety of exquisite floral scents, more intense than those released during daylight. Night scented flowers are often pastel or pure white and are

somewhat tubular. One cannot touch or see fragrances, but it is an integral part of the garden experience. When the sun sets and the glimmering stars come out the night sights, smells and sounds come alive. Take a stroll through the outdoor gardens and witness the white blooms take on an iridescent quality. Stop for a while and listen to the rich melody of the night orchestra; the noisy crickets, the croaking toads and the screeching owls.

Night Gardens
Night gardens, sometimes called moon gardens or evening gardens are perfect for the nocturnal animals and evening entertainers who enjoy the outdoors. Culinary and medicinal herbs such

A starry, white hedge

as Silver Thyme, Mints, Anise, Sage, and Rosemary are the secrets in these gardens as they emit delicately scented perfumes. The Lantana exudes a citrus fragrance which one may find intoxicating or even too pungent. The Garlic vine gives off scent when crushed or brushed. Plant Gardenias as the blossoms do not close at night and will surely add to your night blooming display. Create your night garden with the help of glistening foliage plants of glittery silver, white and golden yellow. Light-reflecting, gray-white foliage of some shrubs are portrayed as interesting white flowers because the leaves illuminate in the dark. With a combination of pale gray shrubs, several night-blooming flowers and glowing candlelit paths the gardener can take advantage of moonlit nights throughout the seasons.

Additionally, with the right colours, textures and aroma you can transform our garden into a nocturnal paradise. The intriguing idea behind a night garden is to reflect the glow and stillness of night-time, to indulge in the aromatic experiences and to create a special area that really offers its best qualities at night. Two shrubs ideal for the night garden are the Silver button- wood and Dusty Miller.

Leucophyllum frutescens
(Texas Sage)

The **Silver Buttonwood** (Conocarpus erectus) is a white-gray shrub. Prune to keep it as attractive by daylight as it is by moonlight. **Dusty Miller** (Senecio cineraria) is a silvery shrub that yields white or pastel blossoms with delicate hues and produces a celestial glow at night. Perfumed night bloomers are popular with many gardeners, because of their beauty and the intoxicating scents that waft through the air in the darkness of night. It is awkward to identify fragrances, but we associate the fragrances from flowers with fruits such as lemon, vanilla, peach, pine and eucalyptus. Some blooms popular for their scents are; the Night phlox, Four o'clock, Gardenia, Evening Primrose, Nicotiana (Scented Tobacco) and Yucca. Others such as the Night Gladiola, Day Lilies, Angel Trumpet, (Datura) Sansevieria and Moon flower release fragrances sweet enough to perfume the entire garden.

Cestrum nocturnum (night blooming Jessamine) is an intensely fragrant shrub. It is a member of the tomato family and is widely grown throughout the tropics. A single shrub should suffice to scent an entire yard. Plant this at a distance from the residence as the fragrance can be overpowering. The night Jessamine prefers full sun and free draining soil.

Cestrum nocturnum

Hylocereus (night-blooming cereus) is a special plant that causes plant enthusiasts to venture out late in the evening to witness the blooming process. The blooms are big and deep like a chalice, with white petals that emit a enigmatic fragrance. Ask for a stem or a leaf and stick this into some soil. In a few weeks you will have a plant of your own. It likes a well-draining potting soil, that is high in organic matter and is comfortable in dappled shade.

Hylocereus Lady of the night)

Brunfelsia jamaicensis

Brunfelsia jamaicensis (rain flower) is a shrub with small, dark green, shiny and leathery leaves. It produces clusters of fragrant creamy white 2 in. flowers with undulating petals grown on long slender tubes above its foliage. Little of its fragrance can be detected during daytime but its sweet fragrance is released at nights. Plant this away from an open widow.

Separate the Scents

Avoid planting many strongly scented plants close to each other. This could mean that all will be flowering at the same time and the fragrances would be overwhelming. Intersperse strongly scented plants with non-scented plants so that the flowering season is staggered all year round. Place fragrant plants where you can appreciate them. Put your favourites and those that are lightly scented up close but save the dramatic aromas for a safe distance from the seating areas.

Some plants are rich in aromatic foliage oils. In several species the foliage fragrance is released into the atmosphere on hot days or by strong winds or heavy rainfall. Foliage fragrance tends to be subtle. There are some unusual blooms that attract flies and similar insects with what we might regard as an off-putting smell.

Plumeria (Frangipani)

Cydista Aequinocialis (Garlic Plant)

Economical solar lighting for the garden's best show

Illuminate the Garden

Lighting is one of the most essential elements in creating a night garden. Increase the use of the garden at night by adding lights. Use lighting to capture those night blooming plants, highlight their performance and to boost outdoor entertaining. Design the lighting and cast scintillating glows toward the plants. Solar lights, decorative torches, lanterns and enclosed candles can also be used in setting the tone for your flowering night garden.

Lighting allows you to enjoy outdoor areas at nights, with no risk of injury caused by poor lighting. It is the best tool to accentuate the garden while bringing out your creativity. Experience the effects of smart lighting with branches, gourds, bamboo, baskets and lampshades. The preference could be the use of sheltered candles, battery powered solar or electric lights. Place these in tress, in flowerpots, on the ground or in the water.

Place solar light in areas where it can be exposed to sunlight for long hours in order to recharge. These are equipped with a solar cells that absorb energy from the sun and store it in the rechargeable batteries. The duration of the light and its brightness depends on the amount of sunlight it stored during the sunlight hours. Garden illumination must be effective and useful, but never obtrusive or glaring. Lighting will: 1. Bring warmth to the outdoors. 2. Install character in the landscape. 3. Create appealing glows. 4. Illuminate the dark areas. 5. Warm the hearts of the guests. 6. Highlight seating areas and focal points. 7. Give dimension to fixtures.8. Encourage the spending of night-time in the garden. 9. Provide security.

Place light at the base of trees

Enhance with dollar lighting

Lighting Tricks Influence the landscape to emerge at dark under soft outdoor lighting and create intriguing shapes and beautiful settings. Nothing enhances the garden at night better than exterior lighting. Change the subtle lighting to coordinate with the occasion, to add instant curb appeal and to beautify your surroundings. Create dramatic, professional effects through shadows and silhouettes with low-lying plants or bounce the light off majestic trees. Deck and rail lights are perfect for a porch or patio. Other lighting includes accent lights and flood lights. These can be planted in the ground or affixed to a wall surface.

1. Place the light at the base of a tree, a wall or a hedge. The light will shine over the surface creating a soft glowing effect. Achieve the desired effect by positioning the light at an angle. The same method can be used to highlight a building.

2. Stick the light in the flowerpot, in front or beside the plant and create a silhouette of the plant.

3. To highlight a special object, light the feature from two sides and get a crisscross effect.

4. Hang the light in a tree or on a pole to focus and at the same time casting interesting shadows.

5. Install floodlight on a tree for security and beautification.

6. Use coloured lights in doorways, at entrances, by the poolside, the gazebo or the barbecue area.

7. Use lights for the moonlight effect. Hang soft lights to reveal a dappled effect on the ground.

8. For a safer walkway, steps or path, use low or raised lighting to reveal details.

9. Light up the water features by placing a light in or around the water. Enjoy the reflections of fish swimming about and of the shadow of overhanging trees. Most appealing in moving water.

10. Install pond lights in the still pond and watch the water surface turn into a mirror.

GARDENING WITH THE CHILDREN

Children love to see things grow. The magical world of gardening fascinates them too. In the eyes of the child and rightly so, gardening is lots of fun and is always full of surprises. Children are naturally attracted to the earth, animals, flowers, bees, butterflies and to the colours and textures around them. They crave our gardening indulgence in which they can participate. Homes and schools which integrate gardens into the activities and curriculum are grooming children who will be much more responsive to the challenges of adult life.

Gardening; A Fantastic Learning Tool

Introduce them early and observe how gardening helps to build a child's senses, develop literacy and numeracy skills and widen their vocabulary.

- They learn the value of exercise as they physically work in the will appreciate planting seeds, watering the plants and waiting for the blooms to appear.
- They develop strong communicative skills and are better able to hold conversations with people from all ages and backgrounds.
- Children are anxious and would like to unearth the seed they planted, they however learn patience while they wait for flowers and vegetables to grow and mature.
- They learn responsibility as they see how necessary it is to care for the plants. If allowed they would fertilize everyday which is over caring and even detrimental.
- Children learn to work amicably together and to share the rewards of gardening.
- They learn to accept loss. When flowers die at the end of the blooming season they are aware that with time and care the plant will bloom again.
- They learn how to arrange flowers for the interior of the house.
- They learn to keep records of plants and gardening sessions through Garden Photography.
- They further extend gardening knowledge to Art, Crafts and to the computer, as they are anxious to share with their friends and teachers their invaluable gardening experiences.

Motivate Them

They practice Garden
Photography

- Make their involvement easy, fun-filled and not compelling.

- Praise their efforts.

- Refer to plants by using their proper names.

- Take them to the horticultural shows.

- Incorporate aquatic life and entice the birds and butterflies to come to the garden.

- Take them shopping at the garden centres where they will see a host of assorted plants, garden accessories and gardening books.

- Buy them garden related books and casually

They pick blooms, and fruits and create arrangements

draw their attention to garden articles in magazines and news papers. When left in charge of their project, call and update. Allow them to plan and execute their parties in the garden.

Make Gardening Safe For Them Keep gardening times early in the morning to avoid the sun. Serve a nice cold glass of smoothie and avoid dehydration. Provide them with safe hand tools and colourful containers. Practice cleanliness by washing with soap and water.

Avoid pitfalls Keep the gardening sessions short. Make the introduction to those creepy garden creatures an exciting one and tell the important role they play in gardening. Avoid the use of pesticides and insecticides.

SPRING-CLEAN THE GARDEN

Some of these activities can be done in a few hours, while others may take a while longer; so let's roll up our sleeves and get the duties done.

- Prune dead and diseased limbs and remove spent blooms.
- Cut edgings and "shape up" topiary and bonsai.
- Repair the garden edges that might have been distorted.
- Rearrange the stones, shells and bricks around the garden beds.
- Add a new coat of mulch to the garden beds.
- Mow the lawns.
- Circle-weed around the trees and garden beds.
- Rake the leaves, put them in the compost and keep the heap or container covered.
- Prepare the White Wash. Mix 5 lbs. white lime, 1/4 pint water soluble glue, 1/3 cube laundry blue to 3 gallons water. Let this mixture stand for 24 hours to achieve the paint effect.
- Whitewash the stones along the driveway and around the base of trees .
- Enhance the gardens with containers of flowering and foliage plants.
- Add to and re-arrange the lights. Repair and replace those that have failed to shine.
- Wash the walkways, driveways, patios and birdbaths.
- Add a fresh coat of paint to garden furniture, fixtures and ornaments.
- Hang pieces of garden art, lay the outdoor carpet and drape the gazebo.
- Spring clean the house too and bring in potted plants to enhance the decor.
- Place tables for the buffet, the bar and drink stations.

HOSTING A GARDEN PARTY

A garden party, unlike a picnic or a barbecue, is known to be a formal occasion. But why not add an informal flair to it and host a party in the garden? This is a great way to get friends and relatives together for a fun-filled evening. Use this opportunity to reminisce and to make new acquaintances. Make the evening a special and memorable one. Host a prestigious event held amidst flamboyant tropical flowers, under the romantic moonlight and surrounded with real Jamaican settings. Why not play vintage music, get on those "fantastic toes" and dance the evening away?

Enjoy the luxurious garden settings

Ample pre-party preparation should be put in place. This will allow the hostess, who most likely loves to dance, the time and the opportunity to greet each guest. Be aware that it is easy to get carried away, so keep tabs on the guests list as the cost of even a small party can mushroom. Parties held indoors or outdoors are quite popular in the summer and on public holidays. Aim at creating a relaxed atmosphere wherein your guests will have a fabulous time. Extend the courtesy and serve a timely notice to your neighbours within hearing distance. Tell them of your intention to host a party and inform them of the date, time and duration. Send this in writing and although you do not intend to disturb their peace you should apologize for any inconvenience the event may cause.

Place adequate lighting for security and safety. The pool should be enclosed or a life-guard assigned to this duty. Ponds and deep water features should be covered, railed and lit to avoid accidents. Some unfamiliar guests or others who may have over indulged in the home-made wines may miss a few steps. Keep electrical wires out of reach.

Select a theme and decorate accordingly. Go sparingly on the centre piece for the tables, use plain table covers rather than floral ones and stick to your colour scheme. The tables and chairs should be positioned for the ultimate comfort of your guests, but not too comfortable to cause reluctance to get up to join the exuberance on the dance floor. Dancing is an enjoyable, social form of physical exercise that is beneficial to everyone. If you love to dance then you are bound to include appropriate music. A band may be perfect for this setting. I recall quite vividly, the garden parties my parents hosted at home where the choice of live music was the mento band. In 2012, fifty five years later my younger son, his wife, my niece, her husband and I, had the privilege of being entertained by the same group of men who played at those parties. They are now famously known as **The Jolly Boys.** Very nostalgic. Wonderful **!**

The Many Benefits of Gardening

It is important to draw attention to the power and benefits of gardening. There are many reasons why gardening tops the lists of favourite hobbies or pastimes activities. This is so because of the innate satisfaction and the beauty of the results. It is the joy of connecting to nature and being able to grow your own flowers, food and herbs. In addition, this hobby offers direct health benefits to avid and casual gardeners alike. Research shows that among other benefits gardening is a therapeutic activity.

- **Enjoyment** One feels better for being outside, enjoying the clean, fresh air that the great outdoors offer. Gardening is a serene occupation, a calm and a grounding experience. Gardening is stimulating as it engages all our senses; the sights, sounds and smells around us, as we touch the textures of soil, talk about the plants and feel the emotions that accompany gardening.

- **Education** Gardening plays a vital role with fundamental skills like literacy and numeracy. It involves team work and societies and encourages much dialogue. It reveals our capacity to become involved and offers opportunities for accomplishment in communication skills and photography.

- **Exercise** Many health benefits could also be the result of the exercise one gets from working in the garden. Surely physical activities improve your strength, mobility and flexibility in the legs, arms and hands. Gardening provides fitness through calorie burning and muscle toning activities.

- **Better physical health** The fresh air and the physical tasks helps to energize the whole body. Scientific studies reveal that simply being in a garden lowers blood pressure. Gardening stimulates appetite and contributes to quiet rest and deep sleep.

- **Better mental health** Gardening improves mental health and promotes a sense of achievement.

- **Relaxation** Gardening adds to the beauty of nature and by so doing can heal the body, mind and soul. It is a form of meditation. It calms the conscious mind and activates the subconscious mind.

- **Provides fresh flowers** Harvesting the food and fruits or a successful cutting of blooms and foliage for the home décor promotes much emotional satisfaction.

- **Supplies fresh food** Gardening provides a healthy source and a wide range of inexpensive, fresh food, fruits and vegetables that are essential to a healthy diet. Grow what you eat, use the manure from the compost heap and home-made pesticide and better appreciate foods, their uses and origin.

- **Creates beautiful surroundings** Gardening is a form of self-expression that builds self confidence, self esteem and pride. Gardens enhance the beauty and upgrade the value of your home.

- **Improves social skills** Gardening as an ideal hobby that develops your ability to mix socially. It is an avenue to make friends and learn practical and intellectual gardening skills. It creates the opportunity to connect with others, thus reducing feelings of lonesomeness.

- **Creates a healthier environment** Gardens are miniature representations of the larger environment. They seem insignificant but play significant roles. Households should follow best practices then the environment would be a much more beautiful, safer and healthier place.

GARDENER'S DICTIONARY

A

ACID SOIL A soil which contains no free lime and has a ph of less than 6.5.

AERIAL ROOT A root, which grows off the stem above ground level. These are commonly seen on philodendrons, some ferns and orchids.

AIR LAYERING A method of propagating woody, single- stem plants; such as the ficus.

ALGAE Plant which live in or near water and have no true stem, leaves or roots, found mostly in new ponds.

ALKALINE SOIL A soil which contains a pH of more than 7.3., other terms are chalky or limey soil.

AMEND To enrich and improve the quality of the soil.

ANNUAL A plant that completes its life cycle within one year of germination.

AQUATIC Animals or plants which grow in or near water.

ARRANGING FLOWERS To plan and fix flowers in vases or containers.

AROMA A pleasant smell.

ASEXUAL REPRODUCTION The division, air layering, cuttings and grafting as distinct from sexual reproduction

ATMOSPHERE The mass of gases surrounding the earth.

B

BALANCE State in which an amount is evenly distributed.

BASKET Container made of interwoven strips of wood, cane, straw, wicker or fabric.

BED A plant area or garden designed to be viewed from all sides.

BIENNIAL A plant that completes its life cycle in two seasons.

BLADE The expanded part of a leaf or petal.

BLEEDING The loss of sap from plant tissues.

BRACT A modified leaf, often mistaken for a petal e.g. Poinsettia, Bougainvillea, Anthurium.

BREWING A method used to process wines and beer.

BONSAI The art of dwarfing trees by careful stem pruning and root restriction

BRACT A modified leaf at the base of a flower. A cluster of small bracts is called a bracteole.

BUD A flower bud is the unopened bloom.

BUDDING A method used to propagate hardy plants.

BULB A storage organ usually formed below ground level used for propagation

C

CACTUS A fleshy desert plant with spines, but no leaves.

CALLUS The scar tissue that forms at the base of a cut.

CALYX The outer leaves that protect a flower bud.

CANE The stem of a bamboo or similar plant.

CAUDEX The thickened base of a tree root of some perennials.

CERAMICS A hard brittle material made by heating clay to a very high temperature such as ceramic pots.

CLIMBER A plant which climbs by twining around a support.

CONTAINERS Object made to hold or store things.

CLIMATIC CONDITIONS The typical weather conditions of an area.

COLOURED LEAF A leaf with one or more distinct colours apart from green, white or cream, referred to as variegated.

COLOURS The appearance of things be it red, yellow or blue.

COMPOST A potting mixture made from decomposed vegetable matter.

COTYLEDON A seed leaf which usually differs in shape from the true leaves which appear later, found in the mango seed.

CROCK A piece of broken pot used to help drainage.

CROWN The bottom part of a herbaceous plant from which the roots grow downwards and the shoots arise.

CULTIVAR Cultivated variety, all modern varieties are cultivars.

CUT BACK To cut or pinch the growth at tip of plant to encourage development of side growth.

CUTTING A piece of a plant, leaf or stem, this can be used to produce a new plant, used for propagation.

D

DAPPLED Mixed with light or a different colour.

DEAD-HEADING The removal of faded heads of flowers.

DECIDUOUS A plant which loses its leaves at the end of the growing season.

DÉCOR The style in which a room or house is decorated.

DESIGNS To work out the

structure or form, by making a sketch or drawing.

DISEASES An illness or sickness

DIVISION A method of propagating plants by separating each one into two or more sections.

DORMANT PERIOD The time a plant has naturally stopped growing, the leaves fall and the top growth has died down.

DOUBLE PETALS Many more petals are present than in the single form e.g. hibiscus

DRAINAGE The process or method of draining excess substance out.

DRIVEWAY A pathway for vehicles connecting a building to a road.

DRYING A method of preserving foods and flowers by removing the moisture.

E

EDGING PLANT A low growing plant grown to line the rim of a garden bed or border.

ENARMOURED Inspired with love.

ENTHUSIASTS An ardent supporter of something.

ENVIRONMENT The surrounding in which people live.

ESTABLISHED PLANT That plant which is well enough rooted to take hold and thrive without intensive care.

EVERGREEN A plant which retains its leaves.

EXOTIC Strictly referring to plants that are not native to the area, but generally speaking, may refer to any unusual plant.

EXTERIOR The outward appearance.

EYE CATCHING Something startling, or beautiful.

F

FAMILY A group of related objects or being.

FERTILIZERS Chemical or organic substance added to the soil to increase its productivity.

FILLER FOLIAGE Selected foliage used to fill a gap or to increase bulk.

FLORAL FOAM Light sponge-like solid used for packing.

FLORAL TAPE A special tape, with or without adhesive used in floral arrangements.

FLOWER The reproductive organ of the plant.

FLOWERING PLANTS Those plants that bear flowers.

FOLIAGE Leaves.

FRAMED BEDS A frame; oftentimes wooden, that surrounds a garden.

FRESH AIR Clean air that is free of pollution.

FROND Long leaf or leaf like part of a fern, palm or seaweed.

FUNGICIDE A chemical used to control diseases caused by fungi.

FUNGUS A plant without leaves, flowers or roots such as a mould that often attack other plants and are treated with chemicals.

G

GALLERY Room or building for the display of works of art.

GARDEN A plot of land for planting flowers, fruits or vegetables.

GARDEN ORNAMENTS Decorative garden accessories.

GARDEN PARTY Social gathering held in the garden.

GERMINATION The first stage in the development of a plant from seed.

GLUE GUN Device from which hot glue is ejected.

GRAFT Transplant of plant tissue by inserting a plant shoot in another stalk.

GREEN HOUSE A glass or mesh building for rearing plants.

GROOM To improve the general appearance of the plants

GROUND COVER An ornamental plant that requires little attention. It is used to provide a low growing cover between plants.

GROUPING Number of plants or things.

GROUPING Number of plants or things regarded as a unit.

H

HANGING BASKETS Suspended baskets with flowers.

HEALTH GIVING FRUITS Natural food organically grown, and free from additives.

HEDGES Row of bushes forming a barrier or boundary.

HERBACEOUS A plant which does not form permanent woody stems.

HERBAL TEAS Beverage steeped with medicinal herbs.

HERBS Plant used for flavouring in cookery and in medicine.

HONE To sharpen.

HORTICULTURE Art or science of cultivating gardens.

HOUSEPLANTS Plants that are grown or kept in the house

HUES Colour or shade.

HUMIDITY The amount of heat or cold required.

HUMUS Term applied to partly decomposed organic matter in the soil, it is actually the jelly-like end product which coats the soil particles.

HYBRID A plant with parent that is genetically distinct. The parent plant may be different cultivars, species but not different family e.g. hibiscus.

I

ILLUMINATE To light up.

IMPROVISED Make use of whatever material is available.

INDIGENOUS Natural to a

country.

INFESTATION Inhabit or over run in unpleasantly large numbers.

INGREDIENTS The component of a mixture

INORGANIC A chemical or fertilizer which is not obtained from a source which is or has been alive.

INSECTS Small. animals with six legs and usually wings, such ants, flies or bugs

INSECTICIDE A chemical used to control insects and pests.

INTERIOR Inside the house or building.

KENZAN A metal-based object with needle-like prongs projecting up from the base.

L

LANDSCAPE The improved natural features of a piece of land.

LANKY A spindly growth.

LARVA The immature stage of some insects; the caterpillar, grub or maggot.

LATEX A milky sap, which exudes from cut surfaces of a few plants such as the Crown of Thorns.

LAWN An area of tended grass

LEACHING The loss of soluble chemicals from the soil due to the downward movement of water.

LEAF MOULD Rotted leaves used in some potting mixtures. Sterilize before using.

LEAFLET One of the parts of a composed leaf.

LIGHT Electromagnetic radiation by which things are made visible; the sun, lamp and solar lights.

LOAM A good quality soil which is not clayey or sandy.

LOBED Rounded projection of a leaf.

M

MANOEUVRE Skilful movement.

MANURE Selected animal waste used as a fertilizer.

MIST Fine spray of liquid.

MISTAKE Error or blunder.

MIXED GARDENS A variety of plants in a garden

MONOCHROMATIC COLOUR SCHEME A colour scheme in which the various tints, shades and hues of a single colour are used.

MONOCHROME In only one colour.

MOSQUITOES Blood-sucking flying insects.

MOUNDED BEDS Heap or hill of earth in which flowering plants or vegetables are cultivated.

MULCH A mixture of damp straw, leaves, wood shaving or husks, used to protect the roots of plants.

MULTICOLOURED A flower with petals, which bear at least three distinctly different colours such as the variegated Hibiscus.

N

NECTAR A sweet substance secreted by some flowers to attract insects especially the honey bee.

NEEDLE POINT HOLDER A flower "frog" or Kenzan is a metal-based object with needle-like prongs projecting up from the base.

NEUTRAL Neither acid nor alkaline pH 6.5-7.5.

NITRATE Compound of nitric acid used as a fertilizer.

NODE The point of a stem where a leaf or bud is attached.

O

OFFSET A young plantlet that appears on a mother plant. This baby plant can be detached and used for propagation.

ORGANIC A mixture or fertilizer which is obtained from plants, birds or the droppings from selected animals

P

PALMATE Lobed divided of ribbed in a manner which resembles a hand.

PASSION Having great enthusiasm.

PATHWAY Surfaced or paved walkway or track

PEAT A decomposed moss or sedge used in making compost in potting plants and known for its water and air holding capacity.

PEBBLE TRAY A shallow tray in which pebbles and water is added. Potted plants that require high humidity are placed on top of these pebbles.

PEDESTAL A base supporting a column, a statue, a flowerpot or vase.

PERENNIAL A plant which live for three years or more under normal conditions such as the coconut palm.

PERFUME Liquid or oil cosmetic worn for its pleasant smell, used also in potpourri.

PETAL One of the divisions of the showy part of the flower.

pH A measure that determines the amount of acid and alkaline that the soil contains. Below of pH6.5 is acid, above pH7.5 is alkaline.

PHOSPHATE Compound used as fertilizer to promote plant growth.

PICTURESQUE A pleasant place to look at.

PINCHING BACK The removal of the growing tip of a stem to induce bushiness and flowering.

PLAN Drawing or diagram showing the layout or design.

PLATTER A large dish.

POISONOUS Substance that kills or injures when swallowed or absorbed.

POLLINATORS Bees, birds, butterflies, bugs that fertilize plants with pollen.

POLLEN The yellow dust produced by the anthers of a flower.

POND A small area of still water that may contain plant and animal life.

POTASH White powdery substance obtained from ashes and used as fertilizer.

POT BOUND The stage when the roots of a plant growing in a pot are extensive enough to prevent active growth.

POT FEET Small stands or props on which potted plants are placed for better ventilation, better drainage and display.

POT HOLDER A nice container that is used to conceal a pot.

POTTING The transfer of a plant from one container to another.

POTPOURRI A fragrant mixture of organic material, dried flower petals, seeds, wood bark.

POTS Assorted shape vessels with space to hold a plant.

PROMINENT Very noticeable or well known.

PROPAGATE To reproduce, breed or grow.

PROPORTION The correct relationship between connected parts.

PRUNE To cut off dead parts or extra branches from a tree or plant.

PUNGENT Having a strong, sharp, bitter taste or smell.

R

RAISED GARDEN A garden that is lifted above the surface of the ground.

REFLECTING POND A small area of still water designed to reflect the sun, clouds and surrounding objects.

REPELLENT Chemical or organic mixture made to ward off insects.

REPOTTING To remove a plant from its original pot, groom and replace in new, fresh soil or placed in a bigger pot.

RESTING PERIOD The time when a plant has naturally stopped growing but when there is little or no leaf fall.

RHIZOME A thickened stem, which grows horizontally below the soil surface.

ROOTING HORMONE A chemical in powder or liquid form, this is used to promote the formation of roots.

ROSETTE A whorl of leaves arising from the base of a plant.

RUNNER A stem which grows along the soil surface, rooting at intervals.

S

SEASONAL Depending on or varying with the season.

SCULPTURES Figures designed in wood, stone or plastic.

SECATEUR A small pruning shear.

SEEDS Matured grains of plants commonly used in propagation.

SELF SEED The natural propagation of a plant by the

germination of the seeds around it.

SHADE Relatively dark place sheltered from the direct sun.

SHEARS Large scissors for cutting and pruning.

SHELLS The hard, outer covering of an egg, a nut, or certain animals.

SHRUB A woody plant with a framework of branches and little or no central stem.

SILHOUTTES Outline of a dark shape seen against a light background.

SINGLE PETAL The normal number of petals is present and is arranged in a single row.

SOIL The top layer of the earth.

SOILLESS COMPOST A seed, multipurpose or potting compost with a non-soil base such as peat.

SOLAR LIGHT Lights that use the energy of the sun.

SPATHE A large bract, sometimes highly coloured, surrounding or enclosing a spathe such as the Anthurium.

SPECIES Plants which are genetically similar and which breed true to type from seeds.

SPIKES A type of flower head, like that of the Orchids.

SPORE A reproductive cell of non-flowering plants such as the ferns.

SPRAY Device for producing fine drops of liquid; branch with buds, leaves, flowers or berries.

STAKE Pointed stick or post driven into the ground as a support for tall or lanky plants or vines.

STEM Long, thin central parts of a plant.

STOCK The total amount of plants or goods available.

SUCCULENTS These are plants with thick, fleshy leaves such as Cacti, Desert Rose.

SUCKER A shoot that arises from an underground shoot or root of a plant. Suckers are used for propagation.

SUNLIGHT Light from the sun.

SURGERY Treatment in which the plant is cut in order to treat or remove the affected part.

T

TAPESTRY Fabric decorated with coloured woven designs

TEMPERATURE The amount of heat or cold.

TEXTURE The feel, structure or consistency of the object

TIERS One of a set of rows placed one above and behind the other.

TINT A paler version of a hue.

TIPS Helpful hints.

TOOLS Implements used by hand.

TOPIARY The art of clipping and training woody plants to form geometric shapes.

TOPSOIL Surface layer of the soil.

TRANSPIRATION The loss of water through the pores of a leaf

TRANSPLANTING Moving a plant from one site to another.

TREE Woody plant with a central trunk.

TRUNK Main part or body of a tree.

TUBER A swollen underground stem which bears eyes, such as potatoes, dahlias.

U

UNDERGROWTH Small trees and bushes growing beneath taller trees.

UTILIZE Make practical use of.

V

VARIEGATED LEAF A leaf with more than one colour.

VASES Ornamental jars especially for flowers.

VEGETABLE REPRODUCTION The method of grafting, layering, cuttings, or divisions; as distinct from seeds.

VENTILATION Letting the fresh air in.

W

WATERFALL Water cascading from a fountain.

WATER- PROOF TAPE A tape with an adhesive that will not let water through as used in floral arrangement.

WATER TUBES Thin plastic tubes used in floral arrangement.

WEEDS Plant growing where undesired.

WELL DRAINED SOIL Soil that is not water-logged and allows water to drain after rainfall or watering.

WHET Increase someone's appetite.

WHORL A group of three or more leaves or flowers appearing at one node in a circle.

WICK-WATERING Watering of pots from the bottom, by means of cloth wick inserted in soil and extending downwards into a water reservoir beneath.

WINE Alcoholic drink made from fermented grapes, oranges or other fruits.

WOOD ASH Powdery substance left when wood is burnt.

INDEX

Printed in the United States
By Bookmasters